AMERICANS
NEED IMPROVEMENT TOO

AMERICANS
NEED IMPROVEMENT TOO

JAMES FERRARI

To order additional copies of this book, contact:
Xlibris Corporation
1-888-795-4274
www.Xlibris.com
Orders@Xlibris.com
31258

CONTENTS

Americans Need Improvement Too

A book which explains why Americans are lagging behind some other countries in education and why we have more drug abuse, and crime than some other countries!

by a patriotic author
who's fighting for a better America!

Written by., James Christopher Ferrari

Dedication

Book is dedicated to the America Indian's, fire fighters, policeman, and average hard-working families like ourselves, who after much hard work and 19 years of 2 full-time paychecks have no bank account (with financial security) like we should, still gave donations to the disasters of this country and others, which show that even with a decline of morals, this country has morals that might persuade the wealthiest to bring back the middle class and help hardworking average families that have paid their dues, to have prosperousness.

Warning, the punctuation in the book is not perfect and you may not want little kids to see this, but words used in the book are decent ones. ha, ha, ha,!

Anyone who is a concerned American,
and wants to see the changes
that we all deserve actually happen,
should read this book!

The Introduction

First of all, let me say that I love America and what we stand for, freedom, democracy, "life, liberty and the pursuit of happiness"! I myself am very patriotic and I am glad I am an American.

Through the years we've been a good leader in the fight for peace and justice. This is why we must remember how blessed we are, and not get too "big-headed"! This book is a critical look at America. I am writing this with the hope that we can become better Americans. After all, we are a role model to the world, and we should "practice what we preach"!

It is important that—We the people must realize . . . . , that the reduction of the public school budgets is a big part of the problem that our children are not learning as good as some years ago. There are less teachers and many more students!? As taxpayers we must not allow the money for Public Education to be taken at all!! In fact., more money should be put back into the Education System, to make it work . . . good again.

CHAPTER 1

The Education of families

We all know that Americans are lagging behind in education! But, why? Everybody has their own theories. A lot of educators say the educational system needs improvement, and this is a reason for our children's trouble in learning. Well I'm sure some improvements will help, but for generations we've had brilliant people come from our schools with the normal school system we've used for years! All of a sudden it needs improvement? No, I don't think that's the problem. I think the schools are as good as they've always been. The problem is what I call "mind pollution"!

How much T.V. does the average child watch? One, two, three or four hours a day? Or, perhaps more. Back in the "baby boomers" generation we all watched a good amount of T.V., but we all did pretty good in school. Now remember, T.V. was much more simple then, more realistic, it was not cluttered with mind-boggling, unreal, far-fetched special effects as it is today! Now we all know children are impressionable! Let me stress the importance of reality in a young growing, learning mind. Remember when you were young and you were confused trying to learn about life? When you learned or realized the reality of something it was precious, right? Back then T.V. was more helpful, it was actually educational!

But now I believe T.V. is un-educational, a nuisance, with the commercials flashing 50 scenes a minute, and all the unrealistic, mind-boggling special effects, it is "mind-pollution"! Our children, who are trying to get a grasp on reality watch this garbage, which is put out by these money-hungry, uncaring corporations! These fast-paced, computer-made, illusion-filled commercials and shows are made to get our children's attention. Well we know children don't know what's good for them. But we do! This "mind-pollution" is as bad if not worse than subliminal messages! My mother was watching one of those commercials with 50 scenes a minute flashing, and she said to me "that hurts my eyes"! I don't like it either. Now, I like a funny or cute commercial and I've always liked good T.V. shows. It used to be more simplistic, more realistic, but now with all the computer-generated garbage on television, I won't even watch it.

I believe with the amount of T.V. our children watch that their perceptions are being distorted before they even get a grip on reality, and I'm sure this mind-boggling garbage can interfere with the learning process. Think about it, other countries don't have as much of this video garbage as we do. it's too fast-paced, to far-fetched, it needs to be toned down. Of course T.V. or videos can be educational, but some kind of censorship is needed!

You know censorship is almost gone. Because of the teenage generation being against censorship like it was a great illness or something. Having no censorship would be an illness! Already people are showing and doing way *James Ferrari* on music television and even on public T.V.! Our little children see this. No wonder teen pregnancy and aids has increased! These people who create this sexual stuff are bad role models. They think they have the right to show themselves or do as they wish, even if little kids are watching. The kids are learning about sex too soon! Censorship is a necessity! No wonder the kids have trouble learning . . . they're being distracted.

On the positive side, the music on television is good, if its good music, I like good music and play and sing, good music promotes, harmony, the love and peace most people work towards.

I thank God, that T.V. was more simplistic when I grew up. I feel bad for kids today, how confusing it must be at times watching such junk on T.V.! I hate to be picking on television, but it's true, there are so many channels now, that they put anything on just to fill the time spot. The same is true with music television. You see things on there and say "how did that get on T.V.?", it has no educational value whatsoever! This "mind-pollution" is all made for money or fame. This is why censorship is needed, to be morally responsible for what we teach our children.

To stay on the subject of videos for a bit longer, I want to write about video games. Of course, video computers can be educational, but they also can be distracting if used too much. I spoke with a woman who was an ex-teacher, retired that is, and she said, "You don't see the kids outside playing with each other as much as you used to" . . . , "they're all inside playing video games". I thought this is sad, kids already watch too much T.V., now they watch it even more. Now maybe you can see why our kids are distracted with too much T.V., fiction, games, sex on T.V., etc., etc.!

In order to get our children to learn better we need to guide their interests in the right direction. We need to make the television they watch wholesome again. Because they do watch a lot of it. Censorship is important!

Here's another aspect, we want our children to do good in school, and to stay away from drugs. Well if they keep filling the kids heads with all these garbage ideas and mind-boggling illusions that are on television, how can we expect them to be drug-free? Their minds can get overloaded, just as yours or mine can! This is where, as I stated before, the importance of reality comes in, to have a clear mind!

It's much easier to "say no to drugs" if you have "peace of mind", and of course you will do much better in school if you don't do drugs. So what I'm getting at here is, how important it is not to overload our children's minds with mind-boggling fiction!

Commercials are the worst, with their optical illusions. There are enough illusions in life as it is without adding to it! The suggestiveness on commercials is very irresponsible. For example, someone telling a kid to buy this for yourself, not them. "Who cares what your parents think"! They're telling the kids go ahead rebel, do what you want, who cares what your parents think! Kids are going to rebel anyway at sometime, why encourage it? Rebellion can interfere with learning. A lot of children are rebellious, with no respect for their elders. Ask any teacher and I'm sure they'll agree. There is also too much emphasis on sex, the kids are trying to mature too fast! They're not learning because they don't care about learning with all these distractions. They're trying to mature too fast and then they think "they know it all", and stop trying.

We need to slow the pace down, kids need time to be kids. I think part of the learning problem is that the children are learning too much, too fast! I believe that we should just do as we've done in past generations, with our schools operating as they always have, but improving our public television, so the kids slow down and don't learn about sex so quickly. I think they'll learn better if they are not trying to mature too fast.

I read about how one idea to improve our kids education levels was to increase the number of school days in a school year. This again would be pushing the kids too fast. They need to be kids, they need time to enjoy themselves. As I've stated earlier, we have a moral-deterioration problem which is why our children are having such difficulty. After all this country was built with morals, religion, it is important that we live by our morals if we want our children to learn and be healthy and happy.

I believe the corporate world is behind this idea to increase the school year, to push the kids more, make them learn faster. Hey, money is involved. For God's sake let the kids be kids, we are only human! You may think what I think is idiotic, but let's look at the facts. Twenty years ago my father in law raised *James Ferrari* children, bought a house, bought a car, and fed his wife and himself on one paycheck alone, his! His wife stayed home and took care of the kids and house. Nowadays my wife and I both must work, (that's twice as much taxes!) and we can barely afford our 50 year old home, 10 year old car, and that's with us buying *James Ferrari* on sale, and inexpensively, and with me doing all the home and car maintenance! We have hardly any money in the bank, we can't afford to hire anyone, a plumber, electrician, landscaper, mover or carpenter . . . I do it all when I'm not at my full-time job! We have one child and we can barely afford babysitting so we can both work! My point is, the government and big business are already taking everything they can from us, at work we have to do the work of two people, like we we're slaves or something, just because of money. They must think they own us. O.K, here is what I've been leading up to, all this does effect education. Because us parents both are working, there is often no parent with their children after school, maybe they're with the babysitter, or if they're older the kids are home alone. No parent there to make sure they're doing their homework, there's no parent there to guide them when they need it.

Now do you see the connection? The last generation had a parent at home and they did much better in learning! Now, the government and big business has, over the years, created a situation where inflation has risen steadily (profit that is), and pays have not! The government now gets twice as much taxes from a family and they still keep raising taxes, business keeps raising prices, while we work like dogs! In a so-called modern society this should not be, we should be having it a little easier, not harder? I read in an article, a study done by two college women, one a professor, that even with all of our modern conveniences, we actually work a month more a year now than 20 years ago! All this that they've created affects our families and our children, their education as well. I believe in such a modern society that we should share the wealth more equally, that we should cooperate instead of compete. Competition is healthy, but it should be done on the sports field, not in daily survival, not in such a so-called, modern society!

Excuse me for going on and on in the last paragraph, but if you are educated, you can plainly see how all competition for money (a mere object) has effected our lives!

If they were as educated as they think they are they would realize that the present money system can never work! At least, not fairly and equally. That money has to circulate, meaning the people who hoard it all need to give some back. You see as I wrote earlier, our present educational system is good enough, it's our country's system of doing things that has affected our lives. I thank God, my mother was at home when I was a kid, I had guidance, someone to talk to about things. That's important. Right now only the wealthy mothers can choose to be a homemaker, or stay at home with the kids. That's not fair at all. With both parents having to work, the kids don't do what they're supposed to, they may party too much, maybe get pregnant or maybe get someone pregnant.

Some of them choose crime! When it's just as bad of a crime for the government or corporate leaders to have created such an unfair economic living situation!

Of course education is important, but for them to want to learn, they must believe in us, they must have our guidance. Kids today probably think, "hey, my parents are never home, they're always working, no one cares, why should I care?" Children are not stupid they can see that everyone seems to be more concerned about money than each other. Do you want our children to grow up caring more about money than human life? I know I won't let that happen. While I'm on the subject of these stupid money-wars and their affect, I once told my wife to put this epitaph on my gravestone, "worked to death for the profit of the rich man". I'll get back to this subject later in the book. I just wanted to relate how education is affected by these money wars.

Too much knowledge? Yes, too much, just like too much food, too much drinking can be bad for you! There is such a thing as too much knowledge. We are only human, and the brain needs rest as well as our bodies do. I can attest to this, because I have become a "Jim of most trades". I have at times in my life suffered mental stress because I used my brain so much, too much, that you can't turn it off, that it keeps running on and on even when your trying to sleep! Then you get burn out! This can be avoided. This is why I am against making the school year longer. We don't want to push the kids too fast. They learn too quickly now. We need to slow the pace down a bit.

Not enough money! A family pays twice as much taxes now, every tax in the book has gone up, but there's not enough money for the schools? Where's all this money going? To the very rich of course! But other than them, there is a lot of money wasted also. Take a look at "The Space Program", now it is useful to an extent, but anybody with any education can see that "there's nothing out there"! Stop wasting our tax money! I'm sure there are other areas we could find lots of money for our schools. The average American pays high taxes. We should not be forced to pay for school programs.

Parental involvement in school is very important. The schools encourage parents to go the meetings or to talk with teachers, but again both parents have to work! So some children get deprived of their own parents' guidance. Once again you can see how this economy has created a lot of problems. I wonder what do you do when a child gets really sick and you have to stay home to take care of them? Does the parent risk losing their job? If America wants to improve our education, we need to restore economic conditions so that a parent can be home some of the time to guide their children.

To sum up this chapter briefly, I believe education starts at home. I believe that television should be more educational. That public television should not be cluttered with mind-boggling illusions or "mind-pollution" which is not educational! Especially since our children who are trying to learn, trying to grasp reality, do watch a good amount of television.

I believe our children need to have a parent at home, at least more often than they do now. I think our school system is good the way it is, but that America needs to improve or restore the stability in a child's homelife.

CHAPTER 2

"Sex and Pornography"

In chapter one I wrote how our children are learning too fast. Well, in chapter two, this is where learning too fast is very obvious. This is where, once again, television commercials, music television, have a very bad influence on our children! Americas "moral report card" is flunking in this subject! Pornography is too much overdone and all for money!

How can America allow the making of more and more X-rated videos and books when teen pregnancy, rape, and sex-related crimes are all on the increase in America? Now I must say books or videos done the way Playboy is done are enlightening or educational to a young man or woman. But all this other X-rated stuff has gotten out of hand! As a man, I must honestly tell you I had my fling with watching these kind of videos, and it doesn't do much for you. In fact, these videos can be as habit forming as alcohol or drugs! I'm glad I threw mine out! Now I didn't watch any of the sick or violent ones, but those must be a real bad influence on people! I did not want my son growing up with that kind of junk in the house!

So who's to blame for this downfall in America's morals? Well the government allows it, after all there's money involved. Of course, we know who's really to blame and that is the people who make them. Like the drug pusher who makes and sells the drugs.

Now a lot of women who make pornography or do exotic dancing, do it for what else, money. Like I mentioned earlier, pornography done tastefully is actually good for American culture, but it's the X-rated, M & S type of stuff that is a bad influence.

Well women are always saying how they are in control of things. I'll be the first to agree with this. If you've watched any of the many talk shows that are about women who do pornography or exotic dancing, you must have noticed this. When they were asked, "don't you feel guilty about taking these men from their wives? The women reply "it's the man's fault or the wife can't keep him at home"! Yet when you ask them about anything else, they say their in control. You see they won't admit what they are doing is wrong, because they are in control! They are the temptress and tempt the men with this overwhelming amount of pornography that is made in America.

It's because they are in control, they could be leading the men to do church work or charity work. But no, they lead them into porn shops or strip joints! it's the amount that bothers me, nowadays there may be more women doing pornography than there are church ladies, and this is sad. Here again, some censorship is needed, things need to be controlled.

This sex and pornography also affects educations. You and I both know that commercials, music television, and regular shows are loaded with sex. Sex sells, at least that's their motto. There it is "sex sells", back to money again. What happened to morals and doing the right thing? You see our kids are distracted by all this public display of sex. When they are starting puberty, they're young, more vulnerable and they need good moral guidance, not irresponsible "so-called" roll-models! They need to be taught about sex in school, but not to see it every time they turn on a TV. They're distracted by all this sex they see, then the next thing you know their pregnant. Our teen pregnancy rate has gotten worse, not better.

This is exactly what I mean about America's decline in morals. And a lot of our problems are because of money. Money is nothing. A mere object, but it sells so they do it anyway no matter who gets affected. These people have no morals and that's why the government should control, censor, or whatever it takes to restore moral responsibility to our people.

Pornography, done normal without stupid sickness and bondage is good! Take prostitution, here again money is the picture. The women who practice prostitution say "hey, why should I work for $5.00 an hour as a waitress, when I can make much more doing prostitution?" Some of these women have children to support, and you can barely afford an apartment on $5.00 an hour, never mind trying to raise a child. You can't totally blame them. Why can't hourly pays be higher as they should be to keep up with inflation? Because the greedy rich people won't give money back into the economy.

Anyway, our government needs to do the right thing instead of doing everything the way the corporate leaders want it to be done. If government doesn't start using the "moral code" again, America could become a "monarchy", which is what we fled from in 1776!

One thing I saw written in a letter to me from a Christian ministry about sex education was very interesting. They wrote, why not teach abstinence in sex education as well as condom use for prevention of pregnancy? Why not? It's a good idea. I had a daughter at 17 years old and that is young, but they're having babies even younger now. After my daughter was born, I thought the next time I have a child I want to do it right and get married first, and I did. I even abstained from sex or "going all the way" for three years with my fiancée while she was in college. I am proud of myself because I did things right for a change. I wish someone would have taught me more about my options to prevent pregnancy at such a young age.

Now they're handing condoms out in schools. This is the parents' job and right, not the schools. I don't totally agree with this action. It's almost like saying "go ahead and do it". Now they'll be really distracted because who cares about learning when you can have sex. I know there's aids, but we shouldn't do things that might encourage them. This country should be waging a war against "sexploitation". If we cleaned up the public TV and limit pornography, then it's less likely that the kids will be concerned about sex at 10 years old.

I am sure a lot of problems are in the courts. A lot of people are crying "freedom of expression". Basically, they don't want any censorship. But like anything, there can be too much freedom! There has to be provisions in the Constitution that would prevent too much "freedom of expression" with regard to moral responsibility. And if not, an amendment should be made. Censorship is very important to protect our youth from trying to mature too quickly.

Recently I saw on the news about a young boy who raped two young girls in the school. That is terrible! I am sure you know America has a high rate of sex crimes, in the world. That's a disgrace! Americans are good leaders when it comes to democracy, but we have more idiots. And again this is why it is so important to restore our morals so that we can assure the stability of our future generations.

In the 70's, 80's, and early 90's porn was at its best! A man could work and then, after a hard day, could have happiness with the porn done nicely. Now some has been ruined, changed. Normal men don't want the, shaving and printed words about cutting tools on a freakin' porn sight, book etc. Some men work with the different tools, and want to forget about tools when they need fun times, and positive thoughts. Again, a helping hand that will prevent stresses! Normal people don't like the word knives on porn sites.

Now check this that the movie with, Austin Powers, character portrays a situation where bad people try to take, damage his mojo, sex drives, perkiness and what a sick trick that would be, what if some sick political group was really doing this?!!! Using psychological, maybe chemicals and trying to control peoples. I hope not. I have faith and the trust that there is more morals than this. I would never do that to anyone . . . poor, rich, bad, good! I would only purchase the heavenly pornography that brings happiness to the man. Again, creating positive atmospheres.

I would have gained the control of my slight pornography addiction years ago, if they left it the way it was. Thankfully there is still the good ones, I had to work and find this. I don't do drugs, and hardly drink, you must have some kind of fun!

CHAPTER 3

"Crime"

Today the Graphic violence is worse than sex on television!

As I mentioned in the previous chapter, America has worse crime rate. Why do you think there is so much crime in America? After all America is a peace-maker. Well, in order to have tranquility, you need comforts, necessities, etc. If everyone in the country had a job, money, food, and a home, there would be no crime. But the fact is that some people have outrageously high paying jobs, far more money than they need. Some have two and three homes, maybe 5 to 10 cars, maybe a yacht. My question is, who are the real thieves? Now don't get me wrong, I firmly believe that a man should work and do his fair share for his fair share, but I also believe that no one person should have so much that it deprives others of having anything. So as it is you have crime. We all have stolen something at one time or another in our lives. Now this doesn't make it right, but if you had no job, money or food, how are you gonna eat? And, of course, some people have to steal to survive.

One way we could eliminate the need for stealing from each other is to "share the wealth".

I recently wrote to one of my state senators about a job sharing plan. This plan would give the people who now work too many hours, voluntary time off, possibly a month or two a year. Of course this would open up many temporary, part-time jobs. This would give money to people who need it, and would help get rid of homelessness, crime, etc. This job-sharing plan would also help the employers in many ways. They liked my idea so much that they wrote back to me that they are working on it. Now that is a start to "sharing the wealth". If the government made sure our pays kept up with inflation, that would help too. Once again some people steal because they make a heck of a lot more money than being a working man. These people who steal are wrong to do so, but the corporate and government agencies are taking more and more out of our pockets every year. They are legally stealing our money. You can see how "money is the root of all evil" and how sharing is the answer to peace and harmony!

Let's move on to the subject of more serious crimes. The United States has a high murder rate as well. This is a serious matter. There are many contributing factors to this problem. Gun control is an important factor. I believe "it is every Americans' right to bear arms", but I believe automatic and some semi-automatic weapons are unnecessary and dangerous, and should not be sold to the general public. This would help somewhat, but there are other factors. Again, I must say that television and movies have too much violence and are a bad influence.

Let's take for example this true story which happened in a town in Massachusetts. A young teenage boy stabbed his girlfriend to death. They later found his room filled with parafinalia he had collected from a series of horror movies about some murderer with the name of Jason. Once again, where is the censorship? This movie and others like it have sequels, part 1, part 2, part 3 and 4. This is sick and it's all for money. Apparently this young teenager became obsessed with these movies and then committed a crime. A person who becomes a doctor or mortician has to be trained to handle the graphic nature of their work, yet these movie companies are allowed to make this garbage, which is very graphic and show it to the general public. The general public are not all able to handle such graphic violence. Movies use to get the idea of a murder across without being so graphic. It still should be the same, censorship is needed. Some of the public who watch these movies and think it's funny or something, don't even realize how sick they are. And as long as they pay to see such garbage, the movie companies keep making them. But in reality these movies are a bad influence. The government should enforce proper censorship. I've seen on television where they do an illusion of a magician sawing a woman in half. They even try to make a joke out of it.

That is sick! Is this really what some American's like? They need to reassess their morals. No wonder there is crime in America, just take a look at the crap that is put on public T.V. and movies. I work with tools and do a lot of my own work. I found that sick illusion very degrading. After a man has been working hard all day, and he sits down in front of his television, he wants to relax and not see some sick-minded crap on T.V.!

What about people who have mental problems already. These movies or shows can put sick ideas in a person's head. So when we talk about crime, I believe we should be judgmental about what our society is doing as a role model.

So, as you can see, there are many factors that contribute to crime in America. Do you realize with this crime we have that people are buying more and more locks for everything they own. Locks for this, locks for that. It's getting ridiculous! If American's would break down and share the wealth more equally, we wouldn't have to live like this. A buddy of mine use to leave everything unlocked in his house, and I'd say "how can you do that?", but you know I envied him, because he didn't have to worry about every little thing! I suppose crime will never totally be gone, but I think we all could pitch in and make things happier for all.

In this chapter I'm trying to illustrate how by using preventative medicine we can reduce crime in the future. Sharing the wealth and responsibility for censorship are big factors.

Here's another crime, a moral crime. The state's using gambling to make money to get by. I realize times are tough, but gambling used to be illegal. Alright, so a little gambling isn't bad, and the lottery is an OK thing, but now they're opening casinos. I see people spend everything they have on games that are fixed in the state's favor. I saw a sign with an 800 number on it, which was put up by the state, a gamblers anonymous number. How ironic, first they get you to gamble and now they're gonna help you. It's like a drug pusher saying "here it's OK to take drugs, but if you take to much it's not my fault". This type of thing is not something to base our income on. The government needs to inspire new companies and job growth. Americans need to restore their values. What's next legalized prostitution and marijuana? It's a crime that America's morals are as bad as they are. At least marijuana is the least bad for you, thankfully I quit and do survive without this.

Well, I wrote in the introduction that this is a critical look at America, and it is. But, if we can improve upon these faults, maybe we can have a better tomorrow.

There's lots of different causes that relate to the rise in the crime rate. As I wrote earlier, money is a big factor. With government in the late 1980's and early 1990's shutting down a lot of public financial aid programs not to mention the closing of mental hospitals, all to save money, a lot of people have been left out in the cold. No wonder there's more crime. These people have needs too, especially the people with mental problems. It is important that they have treatment available if they need it. This help could prevent a crime.

What about equal justice for people who commit crimes? I automatically think of the Rodney King case. Now I don't condone violence in any way, but not everyone is as passive as myself. You take a group of oppressed people with the government taking what little they have by shutting down needed programs, and one little thing could set these people off. As it did. And as far as the four police officers who were seen on tape beating Rodney King, they should not have been let off so easily. No wonder these people rioted. On the other hand there are a lots of good policemen who should be respected.

Like they say, "these are two kinds of justice". We all know this is very wrong. Pay the government a couple million dollars and you get your slap on the wrist. This really bothers me coming from a government which claims equal justice. How many times have we seen some filthy rich person commit a crime, serve two or three years in some luxury detention home, and come out still a millionaire? Here, once again, the government is not "practicing what it preaches".

For people who have committed really bad crimes, they should get life in prison without parole. A murderer should not be allowed back in public. The Death penalty is wrong, even if the supporters are a majority. You may think that "majority rules" but the majority is not always right! Im sure the lynch mobs from history were a majority at the time. If one of your loved ones was accused of murder, and convicted by a jury, but they were in fact innocent, they could be put to death by such an immoral law. Then the lawmakers would be murderers too! What kind of a message are you sending to criminals, when you say—thou shall not kill, but you can kill them? A group of women are working on taking away things like cable T.V., weight lifting, etc., from the prisoners and creating a system where the prisoners do, 10 hours a day hard labor. This is definitely a good idea, it will save some of our tax money as well as produce something by the labor. Also prison life will not be enjoyable, like it is now!

We all know that most of the crimes committed are in the worse sections of towns and cities, the poor sections. Well one reason is these areas have lots of youths with nowhere to go, or nothing to do, and presto they get in trouble. Some cities and towns are finally starting to do something, by trying to organize youth centers to give the kids a place to go. That's a step in the right direction, except that the funding is mostly donations.

Another type of crime we see to much of lately is child molestation. This is sick. But I have to say, that with the huge amounts of pornography available in this country, it's no wonder that these people get sick ideas! I firmly believe that censorship and limits on pornography would greatly reduce sex crimes in our country. After all, whenever they arrest someone for a sex crime, you hear police found boxes of porno tapes and porno books at the person's apartment!

Well, about the only thing I didn't write about in this chapter is crimes related to drugs, which is in the next chapter.

I just want to say there are a lot of things our country can do to prevent crime. This would save us a lot of tax money which goes to feeding and clothing these prisoners and maintaining the prisons.

To end this chapter on crime I want to mention how, if you've noticed, work-related crimes have increased in this country!

Where a frustrated and disgruntled worker has gone and shot fellow workers or supervisors. This could be avoided. This modern day slavery type of "work harder for less money" system is wrong. In such a modern society people should cooperate, not compete for money! These "money wars" are not a game, it is survival to many people. Why make life harder, when we should be sharing and making life easier. We need to create a work system where you do your work without having to "beat the clock". By sharing and caring we could prevent a lot of crime in America.

Last but not least, the fact that it was alleged that President Regan from this country and leaders from other countries sold outdated weapons and guns to some Middle East countries, and they give guns to the little kids who are taught bad fighting, aggressive, habits at a young age! All for sales?!!! Children in all countries should be taught friendliness to prevent wars and then create peacefulness! President Bush also let the automatic gun ban, a 10 year ban, expire and did not reinstate the ban on that.

Sin for sales and the profit!

Doing the right things, that will bring peace to America.

CHAPTER 4

"Drugs"

We all know that drug use is a big problem in America. Again, we need to ask ourselves "why"? And again there are many factors to the answer to this question. Once factor I want to point out is as I mentioned in chapter one, "mind-pollution". There are too many mind boggling illusions to think about! No wonder they turn to drugs, the mind gets overloaded and they are trying to find a way to relax, to find some tranquility! Of course drug use is not the answer, but preventative medicine is! By not overloading our minds in the first place, slow the pace down, if our society would stop trying to beat the clock! I know because I smoked pot fourteen years ago, I quit smoking it when I was 20, and I am 33 now. I quit because I knew it was bad for me. But now that I have a wife, two kids, and a house, there's been many days with too much mental stress due to the unfair economy, that you could easily turn to drugs. Because as I stated in previous chapters, having to do a 40 hour job, child care, home and car maintenance, plumbing, painting, carpentry, lawn work, cooking, dishes, etc., all yourself is mentally stressful! We are human, we need to rest our minds to remain sane. A lot of this needless suffering is caused by the unfair economy.

I thank God I have stayed away from drugs even with all the stress I've suffered. So you see some people use drugs, because of stress, and then again in the even poorer neighborhoods they may use them because there is nothing to do!

So, if you're lucky and you have a well paying job, you've got things to do and you can afford to hire people so that you won't overwork yourself, therefore you have a better chance of a healthy, drug-free life!

Most of the drug use is probably in the poorer neighborhoods. If these youths were given jobs it would help a lot. But how can we create more jobs when these corporate giants let 3,000 people go and put in machines to do the work? That should be illegal! No jobs, no money, nothing to do, presto, drug use, crime, etc. You can see how the unfair distribution of money can indirectly affect things. I come from a rough neighborhood, so I have seen it all.

Drug related crimes is a big concern in America, and rightfully so! Innocent children and adults getting shot or killed is sad. But don't the authorities realize that by waging these drug wars that this has caused the rise in drug-related violence! I know they mean well, and I too am against drugs or drug pushers, but this is not the right way to deal with it!

Education is definitely good teaching our kids to say no. But instead of spending millions on drug raids and arrests and court and jail costs, we should use that money to rehabilitate the drug users. I heard an African American mayor make that statement, and he's absolutely right. You stop the need for drugs, and presto—no drugs! These drug wars are resulting in more violence, and they are not stopping the drug pushers. The fact is, little progress has been made by the use of force, actually people are just getting killed. Little children, being shot or killed in the gunfire, this is avoidable. We can save lives and a lot of money if we help the users stop using!

So as you can see there are a lot of factors to the reasons people start using drugs and ways to help people stop using drugs.

I'd like to mention as I did in the beginning of this chapter on drugs, how important preventative medicine is. That is to do away with too much mind-boggling illusions as you see on television today. As I stated in the chapter on education, our children are trying to learn, trying to grasp reality, they don't need more confusion. This is why I believe so much in the "importance of reality", this country is cluttered with too much fiction! Television, music television, movies, etc. should all be censored to the extent of what is educational and what is not! What is educational and what is not. What is realistic and what is too far fetched. What are we teaching our children? What ideas are we putting in their minds? It's our responsibility. If we teach and show our children good wholesome ideas, they are less likely to get confused and use drugs!

In the previous chapter about sex, I mentioned how prostitutes make more money than working for $5.00 an hour. Well, here again when you talk about drugs and the drug sellers, money is a factor. It's not right, but the drug sellers often make more than an honest job. So, maybe if jobs were more abundant and better paying it would deter people from dealing drugs for profit.

Another important factor in why teenagers or children start using drugs, is their home life. The parents need to teach the children, and help prevent drug use. But again, both parents are forced to work, so no one is home when the teenager is, there's not enough parental guidance! So the economy created by the corporate leaders, and the government has indirectly affected our families.

Do you realize that if our pays were raised to a level more equal with inflation (costs), as the pays used to be, more wives or husbands could stay home with their children and this would create more job openings. With more jobs available, the jobs could be used as incentive for drug users to stop using drugs and better their lives! You see the kids will have guidance and the drug abusers will have something to do with their lives!

In the next chapter I will write about how both parents being forced to work is a cause of family break-ups.

CHAPTER 5

"The Break Up of the American Family"

Here is another problem in America, families not staying together, divorce, children with no father or no mother at home! It's a fact a child with a stable home-life is going to be more self confident, and will most likely not feel a need to use drugs, and they will probably do much better in school. Thank God, as of lately, more people are choosing marriage again.

Why so much divorce? Of course there are lots of reasons, but one cause is both parents having to work. O.K., you're on your feet for 10 hours at work then when you come home you have to take care of your children for 8 hours while your spouse is at work! Then when your spouse is home he has to take care of the kids while you're at work! Both of you are on your feet, going for 14-16 hours a day! That is stressful, so when it gets to you who do you take it out on? Probably your spouse! We are human, we need time to relax, time to cool down, and going 14-16 hours every day is too much! The "American Dream" is almost the "American Nightmare" if you're not well off. Once again, it's because of the unfair distribution of money. Working too much can interfere with people's family lives.

I wrote in one of the previous chapters about how my father-in-law raised four children, bought a house, a car, all with one income, while his wife stayed home and raised the children and maintained the house. You see when he came home at the end of the day he could sit in his chair and relax after a hard day at work. This is important, we are only human, we need to rest our minds and bodies, we need to slow the pace down for some time each day. My mother said when my father would come home from work supper was waiting for him. I take care of my two year old for 7-8 hours then I go to work for 10 hours. I do half the cooking, and my wife does the same. This is ridiculous! This was caused by corporate leaders and the government. It's no wonder that families have such a hard time. Nowadays you have to do your own pension, buy your own health insurance, and do your own car maintenance, home repairs, plumbing, carpentry, painting, lawn work, etc., because you can't afford to hire anyone! They've taken everything they can from the average working guy! It's too much for both parents to be going 14-16 hours a day without proper relaxation! I'm sure a lot of parents start fighting with each other because they're so tired, so mad that they end up taking it out on each other!

I know firsthand how it is. After taking care of your babbling 2 year old from 7:00 AM till 2:00 PM, and having to watch every move they make so they wont hurt themselves, making meals, doing diapers, cleaning, picking up, and then having to go and work for 10 hours after is extremely tiring! You're tired before you start work! These rich people don't know what it is like to have to do this day after day! Having to live like this every day and be a "jack of all trades" to survive, is very tiring and you get burned out. Luckily my wife and I have a good relationship, so even though we have gotten frustrated from working so much, we've only had small fights. But a lot of couples are not as secure in their family life, and being overworked can just cause more problems.

Besides parents being overworked, there is the moral breakdown in America that is also a factor in the breakup of the family. A lot of married men and women have affairs, and with all the pornography and sex everywhere, no wonder they get tempted. Of course they are responsible for their own actions, but there is too much temptation around.

I always disliked porno films and had vowed to myself not to watch them. But then as I stated in a previous chapter, I found myself indulging in watching porno tapes. I had to wake myself up to realize this was not a good habit. I had to admit I was wrong, that is a big problem with a lot of people in America, they can't admit when they are wrong. So the temptation even got to me for a while, there is too much sex and pornography in America. With aids and all the other sexually transmitted diseases, you'd think people would become less promiscuous. So with all the temptation around, boom, people commit adultery like it doesn't matter.

Americans don't realize how spoiled they are. A lot of married men collect pornography, tapes, books, like they were collectors items. Personally, I think collecting things is frivolous. Here in America a man might have a wife and he still collects pornography, while others in the world don't even have basic necessities! Anyway, some men pay more attention to their porno collection than their wives. So the next thing you know, these men or women are having affairs—there's too much temptation! But, sex tapes used with moderation is benificial.

So sex and pornography are out of control in this country, so are American's ideals and morals. Thus the American family has a harder time staying together. Like this one female stripper said to a wife on a talk show, "Why is your man coming to see me strip?". Because of temptation, because her and thousands like her are tempting men for profit. They could be doing church work instead. There is just too much of it plain and simple. Of course you can't totally blame the women even though they are in control of what they choose to do. Sex and pornography pays better. Maybe we should make church work pay better than stripping or pornography, that's an idea. That would be a good incentive to restore morals in America.

Well, I come from a divorced family. My father ran off with my mother's best friend when my sister was seven and I was only one year old! Some best friend, eh! Well, anyhow I know how it can affect you to be without a father or mother. This is why I know how important it is for families to stay together. I've seen how secure and confident children with both parents are, and how it took me longer to gain such confidence.

Drugs and alcohol are also problems that can cause family breakups. But, what causes the drug and alcohol problems! Stress, being overworked because of the need for money to survive.

Again, being overworked is avoidable, with more equal pays, with cooperation, not competition, if we do away with the "money wars", the "beat-the-clock" work situation. Again, I know what I am talking about. My step-father was an alcoholic who abused my mother! After she put up with his problem for 11 or 12 years before she finally divorced him. He was a good provider and a good man when he was sober, but he worked two jobs and I can understand how he became an alcoholic, now that I'm an average working man with too much stress due to the economic conditions. I thank God I've remained sober. So ultimately I believe you can avoid personal and family problems with, once again, preventative medicine by not overworking the people! By sharing the wealth!

In a way a lot of America's problems in society can be connected with a kind of "modern day slavery", where the well off live pretty happy and carefree, while the average guy does most of the work!

When you look at the statistics besides dropouts in school, teen pregnancies, drug use, alcoholism, rape, and crime being on the rise in America, there is a rise in abuse to women and children! Why all this increase in problems in such a so-called modern society? If you've read the previous chapters, I'll bet you know what the answer is. That's right, too much work, too much stress! It's like the little child who abuses his cat, because he has been abused. Because working men and women are abused for profit, they are expected to work faster or harder or work while they are sick, they sometimes abuse their loved ones when they get home. A lot of workers now suffer from carpeltunnel syndrome from having to use their hands so quickly, others suffer back trouble, heart attacks, etc., all because of working to "beat the clock"! So, these people who are suffering pain and frustration end up abusing others.

Before we can have true peace on earth, we first need to have harmony. People working with each other not in competition. The only place competition belongs is on the phys.-ed. field!

Men and women would be so much happier and healthier if the pace of the work place slowed down, thus preventing the workers from getting physical or mental ailments, thus preventing abuse. You see, I keep repeating a lot of things in this book because I want people to realize how competition, "money wars" affect many, many things in our country.

Family to me is sacred. I hope to see the day when family is more important than money in corporate America! Right now the government lets corporations do as they want. The companies have taken away pensions, health insurance, profit sharing, and now have you doing more work with the smaller work forces! Families have it harder than ever, if you're not lucky enough to be rich. So today both of you work, both of your get overworked, and from all the stress family problems can happen. When I see the government and corporate America slow down the pace and make pays more equal with inflation, then I'll believe they are sincere in helping the average American family.

Of course, other than the unnecessary stress from work, there is our own personal dedication to make the family strong. Morals and religion made this country strong. So it needs to be in our everyday life. We need to resist the temptation of adultery, divorce, etc. I myself have worked with the public for many years, and I have had many an opportunity to cheat on my wife. I never have, and never will! Very often in life there is an attraction between members of the opposite sex. You have control when this happens, it's up to you not to falter. After I've seen how my own mother was left, I vowed to be the best husband a man can be! Right now in America a lot of people have strayed from morals and religion. This is a problem that has resulted in a lot of family breakups. Just look at that organization they want to ban prayer in schools and they want to remove the words "in God we trust" from our currency! Who are these people, a bunch of foreigners? Our school prayers and currency was here a long time before they were! Let them move to another school, or another country if they wish.

Morals and religion are an important part of America, we must preserve them as we preserve the bald eagle, to insure the unity of the family and fellow Americans.

CHAPTER 6

"Overtaxation—and Monarchy?"

This great country of ours was founded for the rights of freedom and equality. We Americans fled from overtaxation and the monarchy that existed in England! In Boston on December 16th in 1773 a group of about 50 men disguised as Mohawk Indians boarded a ship and threw 342 chests of tea (valued at £ 18,000) into the water. This was an act in protest of overtaxation. I must add that I find it oddly coincidental that my daughters birthday is also Dec. 16th! Well to continue, I want to know is the government gonna wait until Boston Tea Party #2 happens before it stops overtaxing the poorer classes, the people who don't even have any money!

The fact is while the rich keep getting richer, the poor keep getting poorer! We all know that's true! Are these rich people caring Americans, I suppose some are, but they sure care about their money more! Here's one example, how many big companies made it big in America, and then moved to other countries for cheaper labor? How patriotic! Now you have big companies putting thousands more people out of work, by bringing in machines to do the work! This should be illegal! People's jobs should be protected!

Are they showing concern for the workers? Yet they want the workers to be concerned how they perform their jobs! Meanwhile inflation (the raising of prices) has by far passed up pay raises!

Presently I am working a job that I have at least 10 years experience at. Ten years ago it paid $5.00 an hour, now ten years later it pays $6.00 an hour! My pay went up only $1.00 per hour in ten years while the cost of a home, inflation, taxes, etc. has doubled in ten years! That's highway robbery. Who's getting all this money, and who's in control of who gets what money?, the government? It's becoming more like a monarchy! You know as a honest working American, I couldn't even afford an apartment on this paycheck, while others have houses, vacation homes, campers, boats, maybe a collection of cars! Luckily my wife has a fair and decent pay to keep us going. You know I am professional at my work and I should be making $8.00 an hour after ten years! We all know a politician wouldn't settle for a $1.00 per hour increase in ten years! You see I firmly believe in more equality in pays. Granted a person who goes to college should make more for their extra effort, but a person who has years of experience is professional and should get decent pay even if they didn't go to college! Right now you have some college professionals, like lawyers, etc., making $100.00 an hour while another guy who has 10 years or more experience is making $6.00 an hour! This is not fair, this is not equality. If you reduced one $100.00 an hour pay to $50.00 an hour you could increase 25 peoples' pay by $2.00 an hour! And the college trained person wouldn't suffer very much at $50.00 an hour!

I need to write about pays to show how financially burdened the middle class is, before I even get to the tax part! And I have repeated things in these chapters because a lot of these issues are relative to the unequal distribution of money.

I often thought how does anyone have the right to say they own acres and acres of the earth, while other people own so little. Well I will agree that people who worked the land should have their fair share, but some people nowadays are greedy, they want too much, and it deprives others of attaining their fair share!

I recently wrote this letter to the committee against unfair taxes in Boston, about today's economy, part of it went like this;

Do both of you *James Ferrari* work?
Do both of you pay taxes?
Do both of you take care of your children, when not at work?

Do you *James Ferrari* do your own pension?
Do you *James Ferrari* buy your own health insurance?
Do you *James Ferrari* do your own car and home maintenance?

Do you have to do the work of *James Ferrari* at work? . . . All because of money?

. . . and you're still broke?

To add to this we have a 50 year old house, two 10 year old cars, we buy everything inexpensive and on sale and we use coupons for groceries, and we still have only a couple hundred dollars in the bank! And, I do the carpentry, plumbing, painting, interior decorating, we've done our own moving, I also do the lawn work! And, what do the rich people say, they say we don't have it that bad! Bull! I know they don't have to do as much work as we do! So they think they shouldn't have to pay more taxes! They are the ones who have the money, and owe it! They've taken almost everything they can from the middle class! They live "high off the hog", while we work like dogs!

Recently President Bill Clinton took office. I voted for him and I praise him for his unselfish ideas!

He recently proposed a new tax plan. He said 70% of the tax increase will be paid by people who make over 100 thousand dollars, so as not to raise taxes on the middle class too much! That is a good tax plan, get the money from the people who have it. But the day after his announcement of his tax plan, you see the wealthy people on TV talk shows "crying poverty"! They don't want to give up the money! They definitely fear having to work as hard as the poorer class!, and nobody should have to be overworked! Many people suffer because the rich hoard all the money! Because of this greed it indirectly is the cause of people being overworked, getting sick, having heart attacks, back problems, homelessness, drugs and crime! it's true, money is the root of all evil! The money system can work but only if it is shared fairly!

While I'm writing about being overworked I'm going to show you that I know what I am talking about. I worked a decent paying job before I bought my house, but this is how it was; the job was operating a computer-forms press (making computer forms). It used to be a two person job, one man set up, changed over and operated the machine then he boxed the product, then he sent the boxes down the conveyor to his helper who stacked the 30-50 lb. boxes on a pallet and wrapped them.

Well because of competition, and that other companies started doing it, they changed to a one man job, eliminating the helper! Well their first and second shift operators quit!, hooray for them! Well I needed the money so I took the third shift position, it was mentally and physically grueling work! Besides having to set up, changeover, and adjust the machine, I had to label my boxes then as the machine was running I had to fold the boxes, flip the 30 to 50 pound boxes, cover them, send them through a strapper and down the conveyor, then I had to run down the other end and stack these heavy boxes on skids! Handling the paper and cardboard was so rough on my hands that I bought work gloves to protect them, a new pair of gloves would have holes worn in them by the end of one shift! I figured out that with the amount of times I handled each 30-50 lb. box, I was handling 20-30 thousand pounds of paper a night. I did this for 3 years, while only getting about 4-5 hours of sleep during the day, partly because sleeping during the day is unnatural, and because of personal things happening in my life. My mother who was physically and mentally abused by my alcoholic step-father was abusing alcohol herself and having a nervous breakdown.

I had just gotten married and was the last to move out. I was in the process of rebuilding our car and truck myself to save money as well. Because my mother was drinking heavily and suffering a nervous breakdown, her actions and loudness got her evicted four times! I, while working this two-man job on 3rd shift and losing sleep, had to find apartments and move my mother four times to keep her off the street. I had to travel a lot during the day to put her in various hospitals for help. Once when the doctors had given her too strong of a medication she almost died in my arms at my apartment. I saved her life! She is now rehabilitated and sober and even working a job, thank God! I, however, still suffer stress from sleep loss. This is my point, people should not be overworked in the first place, because it's inhuman, and what happens when problems arise in your personal life, you can get burnout! As it is now you're lucky if you get your four unpaid sick days a year, which is unfair! Now you're expected to work when you sick, which is crazy! You get a bad cold and the employer says take a cold pill and go back to work, when a doctor would tell you to get rest!!? Well, not to get off the subject too much that is what overworked is! Then they give you one week off a year, but you have no money to go anywhere and rest!

So that is why I say the wealthy have no right trying to take more from the middle class. The government and corporate America have been taking, taking, taking for years now! Every tax there is, which probably adds up to 40-45% of our pays now, has gone up in the past five years or so! there is even a tax on tax in some cases! I've owned my house for five years and these tax increases have taken any little extra money I had in my already tight budget. I feel bad for the elderly who are losing their homes daily because they can't afford the tax increases. Homes they worked for all their lives! And SSI hasn't risen with cost of inflation enough, in fact because of the national debt, they've used some SSI funds! Yet a wealthy working person is still entitled to collect SSI even when they don't need it! There is not enough respect for seniority in the corporate world either! They make you do the work of two people now, they make you work like a dog, but then when you get burnt out from working too much, they don't want you anymore, you're not fast enough! You can be replaced by someone younger! If companies cared like they used to, they'd slow down the pace to prevent illness, then the cost of healthcare would be reduced, thereby saving on healthcare taxes. You see a lot of mental and physical stress is caused by getting overheated, overworked, trying to beat the clock. This kind of pace is not necessary with all the people available in America!

I personally have suffered for three years now, mental stress from being overworked! Overworked, because of the money system, trying to stay out of, so-called debt! Well people owe me too, I've worked hard all my life! So because of a lack of money,

I could not afford to take time off when I started suffering from stress, as my doctor suggested! Thus I've suffered more and more mental and physical stress from working when I should have been resting! Now, if I had more than a measly $200.00 in my savings for backup money, I could have taken time off, I needed to recuperate, and I would have avoided unnecessary stress and healed faster!

Preventative medicine! Many, many hard working, honest Americans suffer like myself because of this unequal money system. We all know the well off people who hoard all the money, have money in case they're sick! This is where share-the-wealth is important, also to stop overtaxing the people who can't afford higher taxes! You know, I have many God-given talents, thank God! I've been playing guitar since I was eleven. I could have easily been rich, but I chose to stay with my family! I believe God meant me to be an average working man, to see how hard it is not being well-off, and to write this book!

Over taxation can be a problem for business as well. In my state sometimes called "Taxachusetts" many businesses have left because of too much tax! Which is one reason we have casinos, gambling! Gambling used to be illegal, but now that the government gets the money, it's O.K.! Well lottery isn't bad, but casinos is pushing it. I say that because in a store where I worked we sold lottery tickets, the lottery put a sign near the phone with a 1-800 number to call if you have a gambling problem! Kind of ironic, eh? It's like a drug pusher who says you can have all these drugs but don't do too much! That's where the morals come in. What's next, legalized pot, or prostitution? They really need to limit the amount of gambling establishments they build! The lotteries are OK, casinos should be limited. As it is the money from our lotteries was supposed to solve our financial needs, yet taxes keep going up! This lottery stuff can be bad, because we all know the government is not going to lose money! And they even use commercials now to get you to play more! The odds are against you, so chances are you could spend your food or rent money hoping to win money because you need money! Casinos can be good but only if you can control yourself and actually win, or at least have some fun!

So it's up to you to resist the temptation to spend too much. So even though people do win money occasionally, remember the government is in it for the money! Gambling on the lottery is what they call "voluntary taxation"! United we stand, that's the saying, yet with high mortgages, high taxes, the middle classes bank accounts are stolen, united the rich stand! When the rich restore the fair and just prices, then united we stand!

So what other tax-related rip-offs have I not written about? Here's another one, if you have a profit sharing/retirement account and you withdraw it early you pay 20-30% taxes as usual, but you pay an additional 10% penalty tax for withdrawing it early!? Penalty, for what, it's your money, you may desperately need it! Another legal rip-off! Alright, comedy break, this is an original,. What's an Indian name for a politician?, . . . answer, 'Talking Bull'!!! ha!, ha!, ha!

Tax write-offs, now there's one way the wealthy have been dodging taxes for years. It's about time they start giving some of that money back. And they will if Mr. Clinton's tax proposal gets passed! But we all know the men in congress are all well off, and likely to be affected themselves by passing a tax plan of which 70% would be paid by those who earn $100,000.00 or more! This vote will show the kind of men they are! After all the money system can't work unless there is enough money in circulation, and there won't be enough money if it's all sitting in thousands of millionaires accounts. The money has to come from the people who have it! After all, it's only money and as I say, "it's all monopoly money", just paper, why not just print enough for everyone that does work!, . . .

CHAPTER 7

"Spoiled Rotten"

Americans must be getting spoiled rotten when you consider a country that idolizes movies and sports games which are fictitious by origin. Which brings to mind one of the Ten Commandments, "Thou shall not have any false gods before me"! What's more false than spending millions of dollars on a fictional movie, or a "game"?! Yet millions of people in America waste a lot of their time, really too much time on such frivolities. It's not to say entertainment is not good, it is good, but there is too much! If these millions of people spent half of the time and money they do on these frivolities, on church work instead, our country and other countries would be in pretty good shape right now!

Just think sports games which you played for fun and exercise as a kid, are now a multimillion, maybe billion dollar industry! All this money for playing games!? What a racket! If they used all that time, money and energy to help the poor, there would be no poor! I mean some of these guys make one, two, three million a year!, to play games!? I love sports, and I enjoy watching them, but why not pay them 40 or 50 grand a year? That's what my wife makes as a registered nurse, and hers is a real job!

You see you have people in this country who work like dogs, they work stressful jobs, jobs that are very important, much needed services, as opposed to mere entertainment or games! These people make 10-20 grand a year for working like a dog, which these others make millions for playing games! Americans have their priorities wrong. Movies, actors, actresses are not any better! There are some classic movies that are inspirational, educational, but now they make too many, most of them some fictional garbage, to try and make themselves money! Now they're making movies about almost every scandalous event right after it happens!? We can see the news, we can read papers. Why make a movie about almost every little thing, what a waste of time, materials and energy! It's because of greed for money! In this day and age, people should be conserving our raw materials, electricity and fuels, I know I do. But these people are wasteful, all they care about is making a buck! A lot of Americans are spoiled, it's no wonder other countries hate us! We want other countries to be like us, but we're not setting a very good example lately!

In this day and age where we are supposed to be trying to use less electricity, less gas, less raw materials, less paper, etc., we are using more!? For years now they keep coming out with more electronic garbage from video games to home computers for shopping and checking? I call these "un-necessities", I do my shopping and checking the old-fashioned way. These people are wasting electricity, and the people who keep making all these gadgets are wasting raw materials also. These people must be trying to live some space-age fantasy, with buying everything they think is a needed modern convenience, when in reality they are just compiling more junk and wasting more energy and material! I have a house with the basic necessities, we don't even have a garage door opener or a dishwasher! These other people are spoiled!

With my house and the basic necessities we have, I feel we are doing real good in comparison to other countries. I mean you want to talk about waste, a few years ago they came out with compact disc players, hey, they do sound better, but they're not a necessity! They hyped it up, so everyone would buy them. So many people who had perfectly good cassette players and cassette collections got rid of them and bought all new stuff. I didn't because to me what I have is luxury enough!

What's the newest waste of raw materials?, exercise machines. Have you noticed there are hundreds of different types of these "unnecessary" contraptions. Some for walking, stepping, skiing, riding, sliding. The worse part is that the people buy these things! Why not take a real walk?, or climb some real stairs, or ride a real bike? Do you see how a lot of Americans are getting spoiled, it's like they think they deserve all this unnecessary junk! Another one is big screen TV or high definition TV. What's wrong with regular TV? It's not real anyway, so why should it look better? A regular old TV is a luxury item already! You can see how much money and materials Americans waste. If all the money and materials wasted on movies, sports games and frivolities were used to build homes for the homeless in our country and others, there would be no homeless and probably no crime or wars! What about gas? I saw a television report about how many Americans are buying bigger, faster boats, just for the joy of riding, and how there has been a lot of accidents from people speeding!

Well I have a small boat and a small engine, which means I use less gas! Why can't others settle for a little less as well? A big engine is not a necessity, unless you need a big boat! So then they shouldn't even make them in an age where we are trying to save energy for future generations!

Another waste of raw materials is too many toys. That's right toys! Have you noticed how cluttered the toy stores are with useless stuff! We are talking about toys, things that are just for amusement. When children in our country and others don't even have food or housing, Americans are buying more and more toys for their kids, more toys than they even need. Now of course there are many toys that are good for their imagination and education as well as fun! But nowadays, probably 50% of what they make is junk, bad for the imagination and not educational! Toys that transform into something else—too far fetched! Now they made a toy truck that barks like a dog with teeth!?, how stupid! They've made all kinds of ugly, grotesque looking figurines, robots, etc. The toy makers will make anything that they think will appeal to the kids, which doesn't mean it will be good for the kid's imagination! There was a time that most product names were decent, now, a loss of morals. You see sick names, and sick people buy the trash, then kids learn insensitiveness. Parents should be buying decent products and companies making good things.

As we talked about the subject of education in the first chapter, I wrote how misleading and confusing a lot of illusions on television can be. Well a lot of these far fetched toys also put stupid ideas into our children's minds.

Yet another big waste of raw materials is children's toy furniture and appliances!? A few chairs and a table used to be cute, a little play stove as well, but now they make all kinds of plastic, fake appliances or furniture, and all kinds of other plastic things for the yard! When this stuff breaks it ends up where, in the dump, more plastic to pollute the environment! You see how spoiled some Americans are, they buy all this useless, needless stuff like it was a necessity! You already have real furniture and appliances in your home, you don't need to buy the kids fake ones! There are plenty of smaller toys available.

What about safety of toys? Half the toys out there are not safe! Here's another stupid, frivolous toy that is out, electric toy vehicles for 4 and 5 year olds!? You see them everywhere, those battery operated mini cars, that the kids can really drive! They have all kinds of styles now, and cost between $200.00 and $1,000.00 or more!? You can buy a real car for that! Now there's a good idea, let a 4 or 5 years old drive a toy car that has a battery almost as big as a car battery!? They probably are safe, but have they thought of every danger?

Well I hope it never happens, but what if the 4 or 5 year old gets loose and trys driving on a road? And what about the fact that the child may try to drive your car, after having learned how to drive already? What if that good size battery leaked acid or blew-up as car batteries have done? Yet these well-off parents are buying them up, and when they break, boom, in the dump, more plastic in the dump! And these people who buy these "un-necessities" are supposed to be educated people? Instead of buying such junk they could be using that money to feed starving children. After all isn't a bike good enough for your child?

As Americans, a lot of us take for granted all the luxuries we already have in comparison to other countries! I personally did sponsor a little girl in India, to help her with food and necessities. But because of our taxes and inflation, I couldn't afford the measly $12.00 a month!

What about camcorders, another "un-necessity"! All the well-off people buy them, weren't cameras good enough? More waste of materials! I didn't run out and buy one.

Previously I wrote about one of the frivolities in this country being video games. Well I just want to add something to that subject. I spoke to a teacher one day, and she was saying how you don't see children out on the playgrounds or streets playing with each other as much as you used to? She then said, "they're all home playing video games"! So now they spend more time staring at a TV screen, which is bad for their eyes in the first place!? Personally I will not buy my child very much video games, if any! Hey, he can do that in an arcade! In fact I may even cancel my cable TV, which costs me $300.00 a year for basic cable. Because a lot of the stuff on the 40 or more television channels is just computer-made garbage, and too much TV is not good for you! And most video games, have the fighting, shooting, propaganda, which teaches aggression! This is not good. So, after reading all these pages do you think Americans are spoiled?

What about Insurance Companies and other rich agencies or homeowners, who totally redecorate their offices or homes every year just to change the style!? How wasteful!?, when they could get 5-10 years out of what already exists!

Also they put up new buildings quite often. They're spoiled, and then we pay for it. We suffer as a result of their greed! I can't help but notice these injustices. Another big waste I've noticed is movie-making, which I wrote of earlier. I've often noticed how much they waste to make that, "more than what we need", pile of movies! They waste food, clothing, cars, trucks, fuel, buildings, materials, and of course money! These people are careless!

When are these people gonna wake up to the fact that we need to use our resources wisely? Making a movie here and there is OK, but they make too many! We could at least do away with the porn, violent and fictional movies by censorship! We already have enough movies made for generations to come!

Another problem with the movies, is the wasteful commercialism! After every kids movie, they clutter the stores with more garbage toys! Far from being a necessity! Basic kids toys are all that we need.

But they keep making this junk, all for money! And many spoiled Americans just keep buying it.

It really is up to the Americans not to buy these unnecessary items!

When you talk about commercialism, there is another big waste of time, materials and money! They spend big money and waste materials, as in the movies, just to sell a can of soda? How wasteful and stupid! They could put a plain picture of a can of soda on TV, like they've done before, and it will sell if the public likes it!, plain and simple! That crap that packaging helps sell stuff is crap! All that fancy packaging does is waste material and ink!

I'd like to see a commercial come on and state "our commercial is plain and simple, but the money we save goes to charity"!

Well, when you talk about commercialism what else do you think of? Christmas!, that's right! Now I'm sure you've noticed that the market is cluttered with more and more junk moving electric figurines, more lights, etc. Why is this? It's because people keep buying it! Again, more than what they need! A tree, some lights, a wreath, and some decorations should be enough, but no, not for greedy Americans!

They buy more than what they need! A few lights around a house is nice, but now when we need to conserve electricity, they put up more lights than necessary, put up electric moving figurines? What a waste! The money they waste could be donated to help give needy people things they need! The true meaning of Christmas!

So maybe, just maybe, if you are educated you'll understand why a lot of poorer people in our country and others, think a lot of Americans are spoiled! Because they are spoiled! And maybe the next time you hear a Michael Jackson song, about changing the ways of the world, you'll understand what he means, and do something about it!

Never forget September 1989 and the months and years in that time when the Republicans created "trickle down economics" which increased real estate to "rip-off prices" so high that the middle-class is now close to the poor class, with little bank accounts!!! How unpatriotic! The wealthy administration betrayed the honest working people of America, they started it, with unjust increases, about say 400%, the real estate and taxes so high, I allege some wealthy stole many families bank accounts, and financial security.

CHAPTER 8

"All Talk But No Action"

What does this phrase remind you of? Politics? Nah, what makes you think that? Just because it takes years to get something passed, is no reason to nit-pick! Well, the truth is deliberations are needed before congress passes a bill or law. So you know it's gonna take some time to figure out details. But, the question is, how long? With all the well paid economists and specialists and committees, it really shouldn't take as long as it usually does!

Right now President Clinton, has proposed a tax plan that would take care of our federal deficit. He's the first president who's had the guts to stand up in front of all those rich people and say "pay up"! According to his plan, 70% of the revenue would come from people who make $100,000.00 or more a year! Bravo! The question is will congress, pass this? Will they pass it, thereby giving themselves a tax increase?! Even if they do end up passing it, how long will they drag it out before they do? The newest cliche they are using now is "it's all in the details"! Translation; it'll take a long time to figure out the consequence of the plan. Bullshit!, it does take some time, but they will drag it out as long as they can!

In the meantime, people who are wealthy will use every trick in the book to "hide from this tax"! Those who make their own salaries, will reduce them and invest their money in other ways to avoid paying more tax! How patriotic, these greedy selfish cowards would rather let the average working man suffer more, than help out? What would they have to give up, *James Ferrari* of their houses, maybe *James Ferrari* of their cars?! Most people are thankful to have one house!

Well not all politicians are bad, and not all wealthy people are bad either! I've met many poor and wealthy people that I admire and respect very much. President Bush is one of the presidents I voted for and I liked him very much. He is a family man. I liked his anti-abortion stand. As far as choice goes in this matter, I believe if the baby is alive, the choice has already been made!, by nature, by God, and even the woman has no right to choose different unless it was rape or medical emergency! Even a man, a good man that is, would give his life to protect his family!

President Bush also deserves credit for his good job in handling foreign affairs. He handled the "Desert Storm" war with intelligence, as well as with mercy! I praise him also for his part in starting the "reduction of nuclear weapons" in the two super-power countries. I once had a nightmare of a "nuclear blast", we must pray to God that this never happens so that our children and grandchildren will be safe forever!

Well when Clinton ran against Bush for president, I voted for Clinton, only because he promised to create a kind of "share the wealth" nation, by taxing the people who have it, more! This is a step in the right direction.

It's up to us, the voters, to make sure the politicians we elect, do what they vow to do. After all it's our lives they're messing with when they make decisions! We are the ones who are overworked, being forced to beat the clock, for $6.00 an hour while the highly paid politicians take their sweet-ass time! It's almost like a "modern-day slavery", and who suffers?, we do! No one should be overworked!

Well, hopefully Clinton's plan will get passed, and without too much stalling! After all it's pretty simple, they have money, we don't, so of course it's going to work! For Clinton to propose such a tax the rich plan, he is probably not receiving any payoffs! You know what I mean! These rich people seem to get everything they want, no matter who suffers!

I've often wondered, as I wrote previously, how one man ended up with 100 acres; while another man ended up with 1 acre!? When they were dividing up land years ago, did one guy say "this is my hundred acres, and that's your one acre over there"? Who has the right to say they own more than their fair share of this earth? No one! If you do your share of working, you deserve a fair share, but no one should be so greedy to take way more than what they need!

As I have heard Clinton say "we're all in this together", and that is what this country is about, "united we stand"! So, sharing the wealth is important and I hope these wealthy people are "man enough to do so"!

Well since I had tried sending letters about my idea to Washington and local senators by mail, knowing they may never get read., I decided to give a copy of a job sharing plan to Senator Brian Lees who came in my store occasionally. I figured if I saw Mr. Lees again I'd give it to him personally! Well I wrote the letter and kept it in my work bag, and when I saw him again I said "Could I give you a letter which is about a job-sharing idea I have?", and he kindly said "Sure, this way you know I got it"! I was gladly surprised when a month later I received a thank you letter, stating they were working on my ideas! So I'm glad to know there are good, caring, hard working politicians still around. By the way, my job-sharing idea is described better in Chapter 3.

So what else can we say about a politician's words, besides they should "practice what they preach"? Recently, as I am writing this, I read in the paper that now Clinton says that people who make over $30,000.00 a year will get taxed more too!? This is my tax bracket! Well even though, as I have written in this book, as an average worker I don't make what I should, I'm still willing to give a little more to help! Well this just goes to show how sneaky politicians can be!

So we all hope, at least those of us who are overworked, that our selected candidate will do what he or she has vowed to do. But we must also be sympathetic if he or she does not achieve all of our wishes! For example, our Mass Turnpike was supposed to be toll-free after 10 years of paying tolls to pay for it. Well with increased population and drivers on the road, etc., increased costs, they could not keep such a promise! Now after ten years they need that revenue for the maintenance of this highway.

So there are instances where politicians can't always do what they say they are going to do. Still we do deserve to see a lot more action than words coming from the politicians who get paid so highly!

Yet another good politician in my state is Senator Brian Lees. I mentioned how I wrote to him about a job sharing idea I had, in Chapter 3. I voted for him. It's funny because shortly after I voted for him, he came walking into my gas station, and I turned and there he was! I said "hey didn't I vote for you"? He said, "Well, I hope so"!

When Clinton first ran for president, all during his campaign he said he would raise taxes on those who made $200.000.00 a year or more. Of course they knew this would get him elected! We the average people who make up most of Americans, have put our faith in him. He says now, that even though people making over $30,000 will get hit with tax, but those making over $100,000.00 will get hit hardest! This is of course different from the original campaign speech! Realistically, we all have to pitch in but we'll see if he really does make the wealthy pay the 70% he recently spoke of!? We have to hope that this was not just another "play on words"!

Another thing we would all like to see politicians do to prove their commitment to reducing government overspending of our tax dollars is for them to use their own cars for work like any other working American! How selfish and wasteful for most of the politicians to drive company cars, that we pay for, while most Americans use their own 10 year old vehicles, that they can barely afford, for work! What's their excuse? My wife is college trained and she uses her own car, she doesn't get a company car and she's a professional!

What makes these politicians so special for them to get free cars to use?! Nothing! It's just unfair distribution of money! Of course the higher up politicians have justification for needing limos or cars, but not every politician! Do you think our forefathers planned it so that everyone in politics lives "high off the hog", while the average working man barely gets by? If this were so, we would not have equality, we would just have another monarchy! The day we see these politicians give up their free cars and vacation homes, when one house is all any American should need, is the day we can believe in their commitment to their jobs and sharing the wealth with fellow Americans!

Now the state legislators are proposing a pay raise for themselves. Their average pay is say about $30,000.00 to $60,000.00 per year right now. This pay raise would add about a $10,000.00 to $15,000.00 increase per person! They say they haven't had a raise in about 10 years. Well let's not forget that with all the perks and special interests payoffs that they are probably making much more than their base pay! Now I'm a service worker, and I serve the public, hey—isn't that what they're supposed to do?, "serve the public"! Yeah, they'll serve you if you're wealthy! Well, anyway my yearly pay is about $12,000.00, and my yearly pay has only risen about $2,000.00 in the past ten years and I don't get any perks! In fact I get no health insurance, no pension, no paid sick days, no paid holidays, no payoffs, and I get only 1 week off a year for vacation—*James Ferrari*!, and because I have to work alone running a mini-mart/gas station, I don't even have an uninterrupted dinner break! I have to eat while I'm working! These politicians make sure their pay raises keep up with inflation, and with all their perks they don't even really need the raise. I know you can live pretty comfortable on $60,000.00 to $100,000.00 a year plus! We the people should be able, by the making of a law, to control their pays just as they control ours, after all it's our tax money that pays them! I will not—fully trust or believe a politician until "special interests" payoffs are made *James Ferrari* illegal and until politicians are sincere and humble enough to do their jobs honestly for moderate pays like the rest of us!

If you want truly, a fair government, *James Ferrari* just for—the wealthy, then we *James Ferrari* keep voting in Democrats. And if the elected Democrats are just fooling us, pretending they care, but doing bipartisan votes that benefit the selfish desires of the wealthy Republicans!? Then we have to vote out the bad ones, and keep voting for Democrats until we get true Democrats in office!

Well politicians are not the only ones who are "all talk but no action". In the 90/s you see a lot of musicians who are doing "all talk but no action"! What I am referring to is there are lots of people making songs, making big money, but not practicing what they preach! Now don't get me wrong, I like music a lot, I've been playing music and singing for 22 years, music has helped very much to change the world and bring people together! What I am speaking of is how many of these people are more concerned about getting attention for themselves, than giving it to others!

Now I know there are a lot of musicians who do a lot of good work with their money. But a lot of them are just in it for the money and fame! The music business is getting too commercialized, look how many good songs they use, and put their own words in, to advertise a product, all for, what else? Money! These are classic meaningful songs that should not be tampered with. But that's not my main complaint! I think it's very misleading that so many musicians, who sing about love and sharing, just keep piling up the money and getting rich, but they don't really do anything about our problems in America, except sing about them. You see "all talk but no action", does not accomplish anything!

We've probably sung about everything there is to sing about already! So even though singing is fun and nice, action is more important today! We don't need to stop singing, we just need to do more.

One thing that's bad about how the music industry has gotten out of control is how irresponsible music television is as I stated in the first chapter.

Another bad thing is the kind of songs that make it on the radio! I mean there are songs that have such meaningless words to them, have no value educationally whatsoever, yet they get recorded!? that's how commercialized and corrupt it has become, somebody must be paying somebody!

Well if these hundreds and thousands of rich musicians are as good as they say they are, "let's see some action"!

You know singing about making the world a better place, and actually making the world a better place are two different things! So I say to the thousands maybe millions of people who are aspiring musicians, if you used a lot of your time and energy to help physically improve our earth we will get more achieved, and we can still sing for enjoyment, for it is fun to sing. You know the world of entertainment is much bigger than necessary, if there were as much charity work as there is mere entertainment we probably would have no problems! Make charity work profitable and see how fast it would get done!, right!

You know if the government raised the pays of jobs to where they should be and created more really needed, jobs, it would be incentive for more people to pursue real jobs instead of mere entertainment. So if 75% of the people who do entertainment did "real jobs" we could accomplish much more in our country and others!

Well, to get back to the subject of politics, "there's all talk but no action", and then there is just talking bullshit! A woman says to me recently, "I don't know, they keep saying the recession is improving, but I don't believe it, my son has been out of work for two years!" So, I said to her, they are trying to deceive the public basically, they probably take statistics from one type of job that has increased in numbers of people working, and say oh, look jobs are increasing! Bullshit! Why don't they just say the truth? Is it because they want to quell the public's fears?, you bet it is! They're afraid of revolution, which is how this country was founded!? It's because they have not been truthful enough, it's because they have been deceitful so they can hoard all the money, that this country is having so many problems.

I mean if the politicians lived modestly and settled for lower pays, as we do, if the rest of the wealthy did the same there would be plenty of money for everyone, and less problems! But no, the politicians protect their own high pays, they protect the rich, but they don't protect the rest of us as they should, the general public! So what do they do, tell us bullshit! Like I said before not all politicians or rich people are bad, but the bad ones, the selfish ones, have indirectly caused pain and suffering and even death with their schemes!

Ask a politician or an employer, "how come my pay has gone up only 25% in ten years, when a house costs 10 times more, a car costs 3 times as much, groceries cost 2 times as much than they did 10 years ago"? What kind of answer will you get? Oh, they'll say all kinds of things! How about the plain truth, greed! Why couldn't these people who have made things, invented things, etc., share their good fortune with their fellow man, and accept less profit?

Are these people Christians, or religious? Do they go to church? If they were true Christians, they wouldn't want to be filthy rich while ignoring the needs of others! True Christians would share willingly.

What about double-talk, when people try to make you look like the bad guy! When your employer takes everything he can away from you, health insurance, pension, profit sharing, lowers your pay, and now has you doing more work!, and they say "you have a bad attitude", when you get upset?! It's easy to have a "good attitude" when you're well-off, but if you had to do all the work the middle class has to do, you too would have a "bad attitude"! I try to keep a good attitude even though my job is very stressful at times, but sometimes you get upset. I presently work at a self-service gas station & mini-store. This one is the busiest in Springfield. I've worked and managed stations like this before. At other stations I would make about $6,000.00 on a Thursday or Friday for 2 shifts, at this place I bring in $6,000.00 for my one shift! Now by law there are no breaks or lunch breaks because at an average place you get breaks between customers. Not at this place, quite often it will take me 1 to 2 hours to eat a grinder or sandwiches while I'm working! I have to keep getting up and down and trying to eat in between taking care of customers. At 33 I find this degrading, the owner should have a helper at such a busy place, instead to save money he has only one person on duty! How would you like to have to eat lunch this way? Now I've got stomach problems as a result! He's lucky I still have a good attitude!

Ticked off, I did not vote for President George Bush again. Truth, that when doing management at gas stations I handled the rich peoples money honestly!,. and yet I witness the wealthiest take, through High Mortgages, taxes, families bank accounts.

I guess my point is, don't let an employer's talk make you feel bad, they should feel bad for overworking you! It's never happened to me, but I've seen it happen, an employer fires someone and says "he had a bad attitude". Who are they to judge?! If you try to get something done about these injustices you will probably get "all talk but no action"! We can only hope this changes.

It's too bad that the politicians, entertainers, and employers promise so much yet do so little. I hope to see the day when we will all do more for each other.

CHAPTER 9

"America The Beautiful"

The title of this chapter is of course the title of one of our nation's best songs. Some of the words to that song are "oh, beautiful for spacious skies . . .", you wouldn't want those words to be ". . . . for polluted skies" would you? Of course not!, that's why we must make sure America stays "America the beautiful".

In Chapter 7 I wrote how much needless junk people keep making and buying. Of course economists would say "this is good for the economy"? All this needless excess manufacturing causes more air-pollution, more waste of materials, and more stuff that goes to the dump! So it's stupid, we should be creating jobs that help ecology. I'm glad to see this starting to happen with more recycling. I do my part when throwing out the garbage. There should be some kind of restrictions that would either approve or disapprove of an item being made or not. A restriction that would state "we're sorry, this item is not a necessity and would be a waste of materials, and would cause more pollution to make it"! I mean how else could you control this problem we have?

There is not enough control right now. People do what the heck they please as long as they can pay off the right people to get their way! I mean look at your junk mail, look at all the useless junk they make. Half that stuff shouldn't be allowed on the market! Even the junk mail is pollution, a waste of material! And it's all just to make a buck, a piece of paper! Our jobs, and manufacturing should be based on what is needed, what is good, what is the right thing to do, not on what sells!

So how is our environment in the 90's? Air problems, ozone problems, hurricanes, earthquakes, floods, tornados, landslides, massive forest fires!

Do you think nature is trying to tell us something? Maybe those "know-it-all" businessmen should get their priorities straight! You know one of the astronauts who originally landed on the moon was showing, on a televised show, before and present pictures of the earth from out in space. The picture taken in 1969 showed the earth covered with greenery, the present picture showed the earth with hardly any greenery!

Man has come pretty close to destroying the earth. The plant life is what keeps us alive, without them we would have no oxygen! This is why people need to live in cooperation with nature instead of trying to create some space fantasy. What about that ridiculous "Biosphere 2" project, people trying to create an isolated living place! We already have our beautiful, natural earth. These people are just wasting materials and money. Space exploration is mostly a waste of space, time and money! I mean some of it is useful, it's good we can send people up in a shuttle, maybe to repair a satellite or something. But trying to create some kind of star wars fantasy, is crazy!

Trying to reach Mars or other planets is crazy! What's out there? We know that answer, nothing, mostly rocks! We need to pay more attention to our planet so it doesn't become a rock, or an empty planet! If we took all the wasted money and materials that is wasted by space exploration and used it for our country, we'd have no hungry or homeless in America!

So what other things need to be controlled to protect America the beautiful? Lumbering needs to be controlled so that the plant life will once again cover more of the earth with greenery!

Another problem of course is the use of nuclear energy. We should be trying to use less electricity and finding alternative power sources! They don't even know what may happen, from all this nuclear waste!? They shouldn't gamble with something so dangerous! Look what happened at Chernoble!? I pray to God someone figures out a safe way to dispose of this stuff, like they should have done in the first place! People get big money to work at a nuclear plant, they also get cancer?, all so someone can waste electricity to play a video game!? Pretty stupid, eh?

What about garbage? Americans throw out so much garbage that we are running out of places to dump it! You've heard of barges filled with garbage with no place to go with it!? that's how wasteful Americans are!

Another, very important, environmental problem is the shortage of drinking water! You read about it, you hear it on the news, and the question is always; "How can we conserve water, but one way that we could save the biggest amount of water is by reducing the amount of "useless" industry "in our" country!? The manufacturing of products that are not necessities but are only made, to make something different to put on the market to sell! I'm sure that you've seen them in catalogs and stores, you may have even bought some of these unnecessary items! I personally do not buy items that are frivolous or just an unnecessary convenience! Toys are now getting ridiculous, they have come out with hundreds of toys that are so stupid and unnecessary, they are probably *James Ferrari* educational for our kids! It's that stupid, competitive, money game again! They waste more water and raw materials making this stuff we don't really need, while poor people go without!? As I wrote in a previous chapter, if we worked in cooperation with each other, instead of competition, we could still use the same money system, but more equally divided, and we could stop this senseless waste of water, oil, and raw materials! This righteous "share the wealth" type of government would solve many, many problems! A reduction in this unnecessary manufacturing would also reduce pollution and would reduce toxic waste that has caused sickness in many people!

People need to stop buying things they don't really need. They need to stop throwing out good furniture just to redecorate every year? One solution, of course, is to donate anything that is still good.

Another problem of course is the poorer neighborhoods. The parents need to teach the children responsibility. I come from a poor neighborhood, it was a nice neighborhood at one time. A lot of minorities originally lived there, Italians, Polish,

African-Americans, French people, etc. We kept our apartments and neighborhoods nice. Well now that same neighborhood was wrecked, I mean trash, and furniture all in the alleyways, broken glass everywhere. The hallways and porches of the apartment blocks all with broken railings and graffiti everywhere!? This all happened after the huge incoming of Spanish people, now I am not prejudice, in fact I have a lot of Spanish friends from my neighborhood and I speak Spanish even though I am Italian and French. What I think happened is so many of the poorer Spanish people ended up in our poor neighborhood, that a lot of the irresponsible families ended up there too! Now there are a lot of good Spanish families, poor or rich, but quite a lot of the parents let their kids do what ever they wanted, with no discipline at all! So the neighborhood got wrecked!

Here's a whimsical fact that I must be in tune with nature, because almost every time I plan a fishing trip and backyard parties for the kids. I have good weather, and some friends invite me so I bring them good luck.

Now I don't care what your race is, you as a parent have the responsibility to teach your kids not to damage things, and not to litter, so that we can "keep America beautiful".

A lot of pollution in America is caused by cars, we all know that. The economists probably thought they were smart, when they created an economy where both parents have to work in order to survive, so that twice as much tax could be collected! But because both have to work, there are twice as many cars on the road, twice as much fuel being wasted, and twice as much pollution! Not to mention the added cost of road maintenance! Bravo, smart guys! We used to only need one car per family. right now there are piles of tires that get thrown out and no place to put them! Not to mention all the other junk from cars. This is another problem caused by greed for money. They want to get more tax money, the others want to sell more cars. What we should be doing is being sensible, using only what we need, so as to save resources for our children! It should be the way it was, one car per family, one parent with a decent paying job! And with the other parent home, the children will be guided better and we will have less social problems!

Well anyway instead of them spending more trying to make cars put out less pollution, how about making it so that we can put less cars on the road?

Even if each family had two cars, if only one parent needs to work, there will be less driving, less fuel wasted, etc. Think about it if right now, pays were increased so that one parent could support the family, and they only allow one job per family, it would create one job opening per household, there would be no job shortage!

You can see once again, as I wrote in the chapter "spoiled rotten" how wasteful Americans are! With all the competition in the work world all it does is create more paperwork more wasted fuel, more wasted materials and energy! And the most important loss is the loss of life, the people who get overworked to death!

We could, by working in cooperation, instead of competition live healthier and happier and we would prevent all the waste and pollution we have in America.

Another type of waste, is the waste of time because of too much bureaucracy. Recently, in 1993 a school in Michigan is about to shut down 2-1/2 months early because of lack of funds! It seems the school 4 years ago had budget cuts imposed, which ended the students extra programs, art, music, etc. These are needed programs. Now the state wants to make more budget cuts! Well, apparently the federal government, doesn't allow the state enough money to operate easier, then the state takes money away from wherever they can! Here's where they waste time and money, now they have the whole state or city vote on if they want their taxes raised to support the school! They voted against raising taxes, taxes are high enough now, we all have tight budgets already, yet the federal government keeps pushing off the responsibility back to the state and back to us, even though the high taxes we pay already are for those schools etc. Instead of playing head-games the federal government should just give up the money! Then they would save money by not having to have everyone vote on a matter that should not even be a problem! We all know that if that was a school where a senator's child went, that school would have all the money it needs the very next day! Right!

Well to finish this chapter on "America the Beautiful" and wastefulness. It is the rich and wealthy who can take most of the blame for the wastefulness of our raw materials and the over-polluted cities, and landfills? It's because they continue, to hoard all the money for themselves, that tons of paper is wasted just to keep a record of almost every little transaction so as not to lose any money! To document almost everything for the purpose of profit! Paperwork is necessary for some things, but we could prevent a lot of waste if people just shared more and worked in cooperation, instead of competition, there would be no need for stealing, no need for violence, no need to document as much as we do now! So we can prevent using too much of the earth's raw materials, too quickly, by not making and buying things we don't really need, by not wasting paper, or fuel or other materials. We can reduce pollution, and stop over filling the landfills, and we can once again live in "America the Beautiful", and be a better example for other countries to follow!

A last tidbit, that the fact is I worked with men who did a prank, they thought was funny, actually it was sick! They put animal crap in the ventilation system of a work truck, because they did not like the person! So this is what the sick-bastards are condoning, poisoning for political purposes, what's next?, spreading disease on purpose?!, chemical warfare. No countries, and nobody has the right to do this, I don't care if you're poor or rich, people need moral standards. The simple golden rule, that you "do unto others as you would have them do unto you", is what will preserve morals and "American the beautiful". Making less enemies and making more friends.

CHAPTER 10

"The American Scheme!?"

Well we've all heard of the "American Dream" although many of us may never be able to afford a house. We can just barely afford our children, which of course are the real dream come true. We must thank God that we at least have a place to live, even though many in America don't! If every person who has 2 homes or more, like vacation homes, etc., gave them up for others, there would probably, be no homeless! I finally got a house at 28, but I have to "work like a dog" to keep it! Mostly because pays have not increased, over the past decades, as much as the costs of homes, items, etc., have increased! Of course, not!, this is the "American Scheme"!

The "American Scheme" is a scheme by which the rich stay rich and they keep the poor suppressed and poor! It is premeditated, much like a premeditated murder. And, yes homeless, starving people actually die as a result of this selfish plan! Not to mention the thousands who die from the physical and mental stress from being overworked—just for the profit of the rich man.

Many people are brain-washed or bought off, to think all is OK and fair in la-la land—but it's not! "Even a fool can see"! The wealthy need to stop playing their selfish money games before another revolution happens! People should not have to work to beat the clock, and money should be fair! Work should be at a normal pace to prevent health problems!

What if a revolution started, what would the rich people think? Probably something like this; "Oh well, we don't have to worry we've got the old "police-state" on our side, we'll just have to call in the armed forces and kill all those abused poor people, after all we have to protect our money from these revolutionists!" So basically it's OK for them to hoard all the money, for themselves, no matter who gets hurt! It's perfectly legal, but it's illegal to revolt! Well I am totally against violence, and it's because of us passivists that the rich take advantage of us and abuse us for their profit! But all of us know what's going on, we see the unfairness everyday!

For the average home owners who both have to work from 7:00 in the morning until 11:00 at night, everyday of the year, except for one lousy week off, with no money in the bank to go anywhere!, no pension, maybe no health insurance, for those of us who have to do our own childcare, our own home maintenance, car work, carpentry, plumbing, landscaping, besides our 40 to 50 hours at work, it's not necessarily the "American Dream", it's almost "the American nightmare"! We buy everything cheap and on sale, and still we have no money in the bank! It's not fair that they, the rich, should sit back and have fun while the rest of us suffer!

So as long as the wealthy keep up their "American Scheme", which is, keep the rich, rich and keep the poor, poor!, this country will not be crime free. Because when the rich learn to stop being greedy and "share the wealth", then there will be no need for anyone to steal, or commit crimes, or be homeless, then our streets will be safe again! If we work in cooperation, not competition, we can stop working to beat the clock, we can work at a more humane pace and prevent illnesses, heart attacks, mental stress and crime! If they pay better, for even a low-paying job, it will be incentive to work rather than sell drugs, etc.! . . .

. . . Then we will once again have "the American Dream"!

You've probably heard the song the "The Impossible Dream"! Well when the people of this country dream of a crime-free, safe America, it could be an "impossible dream", unless the wealthy start sharing the wealth so everyone can be happy and carefree!

Trying to make the streets safer by building up the police forces is never going to solve the problem, you need to eliminate the need for stealing, the need for crime, as I've written many times in the book!

So the "American Scheme" has backfired, but the "impossible dream" is possible! The dream of "peace on Earth"!

Read these cliches; "One a thief always a thief", "You have to have a little larceny in you to be a salesman"! Pretty similar in content aren't they?! "It takes a thief", to steal money from the poor!, . . . the American scheme, keep it all for yourself and the heck with the others! These selfish money-wars have never worked, and never will work, only by sharing will we fulfill the American Dream!

Well here's another scheme, or two!?; Take a look at education, education is constantly changing, well when if it's a change for the better, an improvement, that's good!, but when it's a change which makes people who are already certified have to go back to college in order to keep their degree, just to benefit the people who run the colleges, that's just more complex, often just for profit!, just to stay one step ahead of the rest of us! I believe once you have a good system, keep it! If it works, why waste more time and materials to change it!? We should keep things as simple as possible, and not make things complex!

Another example is the auto-industry, once people started fixing their own cars the auto industry started making things more complex so you *James Ferrari* bring your car to the dealer for repairs!

Well this is the way it is in many corporations in America, stay one step ahead, competition, cheat, lie, steal, put irresponsible commercials on TV, what every it takes to bring in the money! What a scheme! But like I've written before, these money-wars have never worked, and only by sharing will we attain peace and happiness and fulfill the "American Dream"!

Now there's a propaganda that is to teach woman and children to be like selfish, militant, businessmen, because these type of men think, women are too caring! These aggressive men and, the video-fighting games agenda, are damn wrong! The road to peace and happiness is the ladies way of friendliness!

There are misguided people that would try to make me look bad, and say my writings are un-patriotic! Not true, far from the truth. Back when I was about sixteen, I did a mural on the high-school wall,

I painted a huge American flag with a canon shooting fireworks! I did this free! And also my father was in the airforce, stepfather the navy, father-in-law the guard and most of my uncles were in the services! I wrote this because the overly-greedy businessmen, through high mortgage prices and taxes, caused myself to overwork to where I'm damaged! So why would I, 'and after 2-pays . . . 19 years . . . and almost broke', support the people who, unjustly took my families financial securities?!!! Some politicians admit that the 'earmarks', millions of tax dollars, are given away to their buddies for unneeded projects!

They might say that the spelling is a little off and I made a few mistakes in English. True, it's not perfect. But traditions' not kept. For commercialism and sales, a good example, the word kids, they put kidz, there is too much of that wierd crap, it's kids this is the American spelling, . . . alright! And they say "change is good", yeah kids but," change is good", mostly if it sells something! They don't want to and many times they do not change to do the right thing! Peoples first, numbers second and morals will help, thirdly fair and just prices and increases by those persons with the controls will help the American dreams to a true peacefulness and the best situations.

CHAPTER 11

"Preventative Medicine and Healthcare"

Healthcare, a big concern nowadays, and rightfully so! So much that because President Clinton said he'd create a national healthcare plan during his election, poof!, he was elected! We all know the employers don't give healthcare anymore, christ, they don't even give pension anymore!? Unless of course you are one of the chosen ones, namely "rich as a bitch"!

Gee, ya know, with the way people get pushed to "beat the clock" at work, it's *James Ferrari* why we have so many health problems!? And I thought slavery was over!!!? All this unnecessary, un-humane, working to beat the clock, just for the profit of the rich-man! Oh, did I repeat something from the last chapter, well I meant to do that! Anyway it's time for a new system, we have to stop working *James Ferrari* just to ultimately benefit a few people, and we need a system where we work at a normal, humane pace for the benefit of *James Ferrari* the people!

So there you have it!, . . . Preventative medicine! How many billions of dollars could we save? How about, how many lives could we save, how much drug use could we stop, how much crime could . . . we stop, and how many wars can we prevent?!

Right now employers, make you work like a dog and they don't give you health insurance!? They make people work too fast, "like there's no tomorrow", which actually causes people to have health problems, like hypertension, high blood pressure, heart attacks, carpeltunnal, etc., . . . then they won't give you healthcare!!!? Nice, aren't they!? Not really, they're selfish and greedy, and their biggest concern is money! If they would be more concerned about all of our welfare, the welfare of each of us, peace in our country and others could be a reality in the near future!

Presently things are just getting worse, a couple works all their lives to buy their house, then when they try to retire, and one of them ends up in the hospital for a good while, with no health insurance, poof, they have to sell their house! Christ with the high taxes and no pension, no healthcare, a lot of elderly people are forced to sell their home when they retire? The house they worked all their lives for!

Well getting back to preventative medicine, what does the doctor tell a person to do after they've diagnosed that a person has *James Ferrari* an illness! He tells them to, quote, "take it easy, don't work *James Ferrari* hard"!

If a person is diagnosed with, high blood pressure, hypertension, heart attacks, back trouble, carpeltunnel, mental stress, the doctor always says "you have to take it easy", so it doesn't do much good to tell people this after, the damage has been done! Why couldn't doctors tell employers, before people develop health problems, too slow down the work pace because it's a *James Ferrari*? Shouldn't this be part of a system of checks and balances? shouldn't health professionals make sure employers are not making their employees work *James Ferrari* fast?! Of course they should, employers should not get away with overworking the employees just for mere monetary gains!

I know, firsthand, all about this. When I was about twenty years old I had stomach trouble almost an ulcer, I was working a lot of third shift back then too. Well the doctor gave me pills to take and a diet to eat. Well my stomach healed beautifully.

But now after 12-13 years of having no trouble at all, my stomach troubles are back!? Since I've had this latest job which is a self-serve, mini-mart, gas station, I have ulcer problems again. The cause is the fact that I work from 1:30 p.m. to 10:30 p.m., 9 hours a day, with no regular lunch break, not even a regular 10-15 min. break! I work standing for most of the 9 hour shift, and I have to eat dinner while I am working, which is very bad for your digestive system. It's actually taking me 2 hours to eat a grinder, while getting up and down from the seat to help customers! The owners get away with this because many of the self-serves aren't that busy, and a person can find time to eat. But the station I work at is one of the busiest in Springfield! At this station I make more money in 9 hours, with just myself working, than we did at a station, I managed previously, in 2 shifts! There needs to be a law that if a station pumps so many gallons the workers are given regular dinner breaks! Even after my doctor gave me a note for my employer stating that I need at least a half hour *James Ferrari* dinner break, my employer only lets me sit down long enough to eat, about 5-10 minutes, only on Thursdays and Fridays, and then it's right back to work! This is inhumane!

He says he can't afford to have someone work a half hour to give me a dinner break? Yeah, right, like I should feel sorry for him, when I'm the sick one! You see, how being overworked can cause health problems! The gas business is one of the most profitable type of business, and yet here they are crying poverty, and abusing their employees!? Such a profitable business *James Ferrari* get away with *James Ferrari* giving uninterrupted breaks for dinner during 9 hour shifts!

I am 33 years old, and I don't even have a dinner break at work! talk about no respect! It used to be that as you got older you would get more benefits as you get seniority, but now they take more and more away from you!? And as you get older, if you can't keep a fast pace, they get rid of you and replace you with a younger person! "The employers want you to work hard and care about them, but they don't care about you"! "Obviously when people get older they slow down and that should not threaten anyone's job security"!

There should be a system by which as people get older that they gradually make more money for their seniority and knowledge. At my age I am only making $1.00 more, per hour than I did *10* years ago! and I have no dinner break! As we get older we have more responsibility so we need better compensation. I have a wife, two kids and a house to take care of! Thank God, my wife makes a *James Ferrari* paycheck as an RN! Sure teenagers should start low in the work place $5-6 an hour, they have less responsibility, but as we get older we need fair increases to survive. As an honest working person I couldn't even afford an apartment on my paycheck alone! That's bad, and it's because of unfair inflation! So if we made a system which increased our pays with seniority, how would we pay for it? "By taking from the rich and giving to the poor!" Basically if we limited the amount any one person could make, which would create a lot of extra money, for others! I know the first thing you'd hear out of a rich person's mouth would be "that's an infringement on my freedom to make as much as I want", but the reality is that there are already limitations on what we make, one way or another!

And the saying, "You can never have too much money," is wrong . . . , just like too much drugs and alcohol, too much money, greed can turn some people bad, and create added problems.

The limitations are by the government, taxes, the guy or woman at the top who limits your yearly income, the consumers who effect profits by what they purchase, so there are limitations already! So if we create more equal and fair pays and slow down the work pace we will prevent many illnesses! Did 'ya ever notice how healthy the rich people are and how there is much more sickness among the poor who are overworked? Sometimes you hear a person say, "doesn't that actress look young and healthy for being 40 years old?' Well of course they stay young and healthy, they "live the life of Riley"! They *James Ferrari* overworked, and they get plenty of vacation time! Besides that they are rich, pampered and definitely get the best healthcare. An entertainer should not make any more than a registered nurse, for the nurse does a much more important service. There would be plenty of money for everyone if the rich didn't hoard it all! In order for people to be healthier we all need more equal and fair pays! And plenty of vacation time as well!

What about sick time? I know many people have sick days they can use at work, but the majority of us don't have any paid sick days!? Here is another benefit the employers have taken from us! You know the pharmaceutical companies make all kinds of cold pills to control your cold symptoms, this way here, you can still go to work when you're sick! Oh, whoopee-do! You know when you come down with a bad cold, if you go to see your doctor he or she says "you should stay home and rest"!, but your employer says "oh, just take a cold pill, and go back to work"!? Awful nice of them, eh?

Years of pushing yourself like this when you're sick must take a toll on a person eventually. Another cause of health problems is sleep deprivation. People who work third shift for a number of years and lose sleep because of the difficulty in sleeping during the day! You work 8-10 hours all night then sleep 4-6 hours, if you're lucky, which is not good for you! Over the years this sleep loss can add up! By nature, most humans sleep best at night. I know I've done 5-6 years of third shift work and I've lost a lot of sleep because of it! Now you see television programs where doctors are saying how working third shift is a health risk, because of the sleep loss! Wow, they're just finding this out!?

It amazes me that they always seem to discover these problems 30 or 40 years after the fact! I mean they wait till, hundreds of thousands of people, who have been suffering for years, finally complain about their sleep loss before they do something about it! Obviously, employers and doctors have known about these health risks for years! Now some people are able to work third shift and still sleep good during the day, but for most people it's not good for them. So it would be nice if, unless it be an important necessity like guard duty, etc., that they would limit the use of third shifts. Or, at least give people different shifts at 3 month intervals, or something, allowing them proper rest! We really need a doctor's system of checks and balances, where doctors make sure employees are not overworked. But in order for this ever to become a reality, people's health needs to be a primary concern, and profit secondary!

People need to realize that preventative medicine is very important. Personally, I've suffered *James Ferrari* mental stress as a result of having to learn so many different trades to survive! It should be like it was before, a person learns 3 or 4 trades, and gets paid fairly, and that's all the knowledge they need for their survival. Because like too much of anything, too much knowledge is bad, and the brain thinks too much!

And when the brain thinks too much, you get *James Ferrari*, and when that happens you start having abnormal thoughts! So why has there been more and more murders, and suicides, and people going bizerk and going on a killing rampage!? Because people are snapping! They are being so overworked, with both parents having to work, having to do the work of *James Ferrari* people at work, etc. You always hear of postal workers, how come? Because that's one of the fastest paced type of work, it's very stressful. They pay $10-15 an hour but you work like a dog if you're sorting mail or something! I know I worked in the paper factory, and that is even harder work!

So preventing mental and physical stress is important in preventing crime!

I've said it before, we need to slow down the work pace to a humane pace!

I recently wrote this letter to an organization for treatment of abused women. The reason I wrote the letter is because people are wondering why there is an increase in abuse in families. Well this is a mental health issue and here's what I wrote;

June 10, 1993

To Whom It May Concern:

I firmly believe that our present, unequal money system is the cause of many of our physical and emotional, and social problems, namely stress, heartattacks, drug use, alcoholism, physical abuse, and crime! And I believe the people who control money distribution are responsible for keeping the rich, rich and keeping the poor, poor! So obviously these people are indirectly responsible for the problems that the poorer people develop over the years by having to work at an inhumane pace, trying to "beat the clock", just for the profit of the rich man! While the average worker is constantly being overworked just to barely survive!

Just like a child who is abused, and the child then abuses his pet kitten, so is the average worker who is constantly overwhelmed and used and abused in his fight to maintain his financial security! This, once normal person, may eventually develop physical or mental problems and may even abuse others!

I know, firsthand, what it's like to struggle to survive. I come from the poor part of Holyoke. My stepfather who was an alcoholic, abused my mother. Though I always protected my mother, I understood why my stepfather had these problems.

He was a good man when he was sober, and a good provider, he worked two jobs, machinery and carpentry, the kind of hard work most rich people wouldn't want to have to do for 30-40 years! He must have had a lot of anger inside himself from being used and abused which he in turn let out on my mother. I am totally against violence, but this is why it happens!

My wife and I now own a home, it's a 50 year old home. We both work, both pay taxes, we both have to take care of our son when we are not at our full-time jobs. We own 2 ten year old vehicles, we buy everything cheap and on sale! We do our own cooking and house cleaning When we moved, we did our own moving, and interior decorating. I have to do my own home maintenance, carpentry, electrical, plumbing and I do most of our auto repairs! And I do my own lawn work too! We do all this work, and we still don't have any money in the bank, only a couple hundred dollars!? We can't afford to hire others to do some of this work. We can't even afford much babysitting! Do you have to do this much work? Not if you're wealthy, right! I don't even get a week of paid vacation at my job, and we couldn't afford to go anywhere if I did!!

This is an unequal money system! Until the wealthy stop being greedy, and learn to "share the wealth", there will still be many problems in our country! We have to live in cooperation with each other, not so much competition. Leave competition for the sports field. In such a "so-called" modern society, we should not have so much crime, or so many problems. These problems are mostly a result of these selfish money-wars!

I am working a job, that presently, pays about a buck more an hour than this same job paid 10 years ago! While the cost of homes has doubled from 50 grand to 100 grand in 10 years!? And everything else has doubled and tripled in price except our pays! I've worked many jobs, when I was making $10.00 an hour, I had to do the work that 2 people used to do! Because of the economy, many people are now doing the work of 2 people, but getting no more money for it!?

I get up at 7:00 every morning, watch my 3 year old from 7:00 a.m. till 1:00 p.m., then I go to work from 1:30 p.m. till 11:00 p.m., and I go to sleep at 11:30 or 12:00! That's 14-16 hours everyday, and my wife does the same! This causes hypertension, mental stress! You must realize, just like too much of anything . . . too much working, or too much use of the brain can be bad for you! I have suffered physical and mental stress, I thank God I'm a passive man, it's the ones who aren't so passive that end up abusing their families or going out and shooting someone! And you wonder why abuse against women, child abuse, and crime are on the rise?!

Last year, I read an article in the Springfield paper, where 2 college women, one a professor, wrote in a study that, even with modern conveniences, we actually work a month more a year than 20 years ago!? In Sweden, I think it was, they wrote, no matter what kind of job you do, you get a month off every year! I'll bet they're a lot healthier and happier too!

I personally handed a letter to Senator Brian Lees about a job-sharing plan which would, by choice, give the people who work too much, time off, and put the people who don't have work, to work! But besides this, pay scales need to be made more equal, college or no college! Yes, a college person should make more, but not 2, 3 & 4 times as much per hour, when average workers are professionals at their jobs too!

Sincerely,
James Christopher Ferrari

Now I wrote this letter and sent copies to news organizations hoping they would research this or do a story so as to correct these injustices which eventually cause mental or physical problems! I also wrote this next letter which I also sent out to news stations and television stations, concerning the mental stress which comes from watching too much man-made, computer-made illusions on commercials, and TV shows, I call it "mind-pollution"! Here's what I wrote;

June, 1993

To Whom It May Concern:

I am very concerned about the direction many of the people in our country have taken, which is to except and condone uncensored commercials, television, music-television and movies!? Let me point out that at a time when we are trying to create a drug-free, crime-free America, in reality, with the mind-boggling illusions, and crime, and sex shown on television, it causes more mental instability and confusion in the minds of children and adults which could cause drug abuse or crime! You must realize that people are striving to grasp reality, especially children whose young minds are still trying to figure out the real world, and flashing some unreal, mind-boggling illusions on a commercial, can cause confusion! I call it mind-pollution! Commercials, TV, movies, used to be more simple and enjoyable, but now I won't even watch movies, I hate most commercials, and I won't even watch music-television even though I am a musician! My mother was recently watching a commercial, flashing 50 scenes a minute, and she said to me, "that hurts my eyes!" She doesn't like TV anymore either! If we keep allowing the media, to put stupid ideas in our kids heads, they are going to keep using drugs!

I saw a senator on C-span, talking about this problem and how our children spend more time watching TV than they do in school! Which obviously means the programs better be wholesome, educational stuff. This senator went on to say he didn't think censorship is the answer, he said more information on the content would work? That's bull, you have no way of knowing what the next commercial will be, or if it will be within the realm of reality! The truth is nobody wants to confront these wealthy advertisers? Censorship worked before and it will work again. There was censorship when I grew up, and TV was much more simplistic, with less graphic scenes, and less computer made illusions, it was definitely less harmful to the mind!

Now I am an average home-owner, I work 45 hours a week, my wife and I both take care of our son when we're not at work. I get up at 7:00 a.m. everyday, from 7:00 a.m. till 2:00 p.m I take care of my son, from 2:00 p.m. till 11:00 p.m. I work, that's 16 hours a day! Now because of inflation I do my own home maintenance, carpentry, plumbing, electrical, my own car work, my own landscaping, lawn care, etc.! By the end of the day my brain is burnt out. When I do get to sit in my chair and watch a little TV, the last thing I want to see is some mind-boggling commercial, or television show when my mind is so tired! It causes mental anxiety! It's a wonder that I don't do drugs or drink heavily!

So why does America have more drug use and crime than most other countries?! Obviously because Americans create more useless fiction, illusions, violence, mind-pollution than most other countries! Too much illusion is bad for you, just like too much of anything, too much drinking, too much drugs, etc.!

You need to realize these commercials and shows with the illusions which are too far-fetched, are made to attract our children's attention. Sure the kids may laugh at it because they don't know better, they don't know what's good for them! But, the parents do! And I would say most parents do not like the garbage the television industry creates.

Go ahead take a poll of parents and adults, 30 and over, experienced adults, I'll bet most of them don't like too much illusion!

Personally, because I have a vivid imagination, and such a good memory, and I am often over-tired, have suffered mental stress because of stupid thoughts caused by some, unreal, far-fetched, illusion, I'd seen on television! This is needless and preventable!!!

My only hope is that, the politicians who get paid so well, will stop being so concerned about the desires of these people with all the money, namely the advertisers and television industry, and that they will do their jobs correctly, and enforce some censorship, to ensure some degree of mentally healthy, educational television.

Sincerely,
James Christopher Ferrari

P.S. You must realize that people who have developed physical or mental problems, over the years, do not need this kind of careless, irresponsible television to add to their problems!

P.S.S. I personally will cancel cable if things do not improve, I will not spend $250.00 a year or more for such garbage!

I've been writing these letters, with hopes that people will get smart and make the changes necessary to make a healthier and happier America!

I would like for it to be known, that this is also the reason I have written this book!

If you keep damaging the angels, what is left? And if you kill the peace movement, what then is left?

What do you create?

I create much heaven and create as much as possible, the atmosphere where children will learn the friendliest habits, living with happiness.

And this prevents stress!!!

I am living proof, the baby boomers as children, grew up with, less graphic TV, and more morals, gentlemen.

This could be prevented, that too many changes have been made for some kind of psychological, commercialism. Where they've made some stores more annoying, for 30-40 years most businesses and department stores had instrumental type music, a tried and true music that most people like, now has been changed, to music with words. After dealing with noisy kids all day, I don't want to hear noisy words while I'm trying to shop. I like music but if I want music I go to a club. At the stores it's just annoying commercialism at its worse! I was bothered from whatever crap they blasted, I walked out of stores 70 times, bought nothing, even wrote and told them this! And using good songs for a burger commercial is wrong. Let them write their own jingles, a love song should be kept sacred for future kids and some people cherish a song from weddings. Like too much drugs, commercialism has gone stupid

CHAPTER 12

A living history of the next 10 years

This book was written, at least the first 11 chapters, about 1996 and now it is Feb., 2004! So I rounded off the numbers to make a decade! I have not yet been able to publish this book because of a lack of money, repression, lack of time, and illness from the overload and stress! The problem with this, the monarchies premeditated plan to overwork the average people with misuse of the controls they possess, to hoard let's say 75% of the riches, and prevent protest, cause people are too busy, is they help damage good people in the process and alter the evolution of peacefulness! As many "average Americans" know in "rip-off" economy! Ten years after this country has gotten worse!!!

We now have "Enron", which the supposed good guy new President George W. Bush, is alleged to have connections with! Enron or its accounting firm is alleged to steal the retirement money of hundreds of trusting people!!!, through deceptive false numbers!

Then, September 11th happens, the two money-towers are attacked and many innocent people and not so innocent are killed! How tragic! All this violence over money and "so-called" power! Violence is never the answer but greedy-selfishness is almost as bad! Which proves . . . . , global-competition should be; global cooperation with the peoples! Leave competition to the sports field. Life is not a game, life is real!, and deserves the most priorities!

So we know what the next thing is. We counter-attack
Afghanistan, which I supported President George W. Bush and
Powel, etc., because this is truly a security issue, to defend America
from any attacking countries!

But before the job is finished, they forget Bin laddin and decide
to do a preemptive strike on Iraq, attack and invade a country that
is weak and been sanctioned for 10 years!? Why? . . . , for oil and
land position?, and business?! The war could have been a short air
battle in a small country, instead they put it on the ground.

I would never believe that our country is capable of such
conspiracy until I watched, and then bought a copy of tapes, from
the "History channel". This is about one of our greatest presidents,
John F. Kennedy, who avoided a nuclear-war!!!

This is about facts, that John F. Kennedy was trying to stop the
Vietnam War and have 1000 troops home by Christmas and that
he had signed a document to that effect! The giant multi-million
dollar oil companies, and military industries did not like this! It
is alleged, numerous security breeches occurred in Texas, inside
strings had to be pulled, when our president was assassinated!!! It
only took a few, high position men to do this! Most of the policeman
and security people did what they were told, through orders from
those in control! I am sad for the loss, John F. Kennedy, was one of
the best! After President George W. Bush and his administration
attacked Iraq, killing thousands of innocent, and not so innocent
people, if you noticed, we had some of the worst weather, many
snow-storms and like a year of rain and hurricanes! We need
leaders who are experienced, and will protect the innocent people
living in countries, I say elect John F. Kerry for president.

After Kennedy, then Johnson was sworn in as president, he was
friends with some millionaire oil-tycoons, and the war in Vietnam
continued for Approx. 17 yrs!, and approximately 58,000 men were
killed!!! The industrial and oil companies made millions of dollars?!
These overly-greedy conspirators, and tycoons thought they got
rid of John F. Kennedy, but in fact the goodness of his presidential
deeds and actions and his spiritualness has a powerfulness that is
timeless!!!

So now after this bit of history I know that most likely the attack on Iraq was for oil and profit!!! Here's the letter that I wrote on April 14 2003;

Dear Senator John Kerry,

'Time to get a "regime-change" for us! And please feel free to use anything from this letter for your campaign! I've watched this invasion, they goofed!, they should have named that 'operation oil-well', because you know Mr. George isn't spending 100 billion of our tax-dollars just to free Iraqis! He wouldn't spend that much for us! My guess is that they'll never find Saddam dead, because to admit that our in-compitent president would be accused of assasination! War declaration is a last resort, I feel sorry for all the innocent killed on both sides. Mr. Georges' bad decision has determined the fate of many people . . . , and he's far from god! Even the well-educated and elder historians have condemned this! To set the example to other countries that Republicans are on an imperialistic business-venture, destroying and rebuilding for profit, which is what this looks like, is making more enemies who may try the same thing! My father was in the airforce, and my step-father was in the navy! And I know about 'honorable-wars", this action was a disgrace and the wealthy who wanted this slaughter should be the ones to pay for that. Most of the people did not want to invade, but to let Hussien make the first mistake!

What was seen on main-stream media is that the actions of our present leaders and the Iraqis leaders are not much different in this 'stupid money-power pursuit'!

Thier country; use gun threats to force some men to fight,
   Restrict the media,
   Gas and kill thousands of thier people.

Our country;   , is more humane,

>The threat of prison to draft and force men to fight in some wars like Vietnam,
>
>Military restricts media to downplay 115,000 + civilians killed in Iraq
>
>Bomb and destroy thousands of people

And how many businessmen lost their livelihoods to bombs and looting? A tell-tail sign of the true agenda was no protection of Iraq's ancient treasures, but that oil was protected first-thing! This was never about the liberation of peoples lives. This was to capitalize with use of force and freedom just happens to be a benefit! But only a percentage are for this.

So I wrote this that you will know that majorities of people are against this alleged land-grab and war for profit!? You know seeing Americans watch a war like it was a football game and cheering while innocent women and children were killed is sick! I don't blame the soldiers who are pawns! But the so-called leaders who attack and kill will get paid (just like Iraqis), and live an easier life than people who push for peacefulness!

How ironic, while George and his cronies were part of bombing and crippling people, I, for approx., about the last 4 months have been transporting and helping the disabled people in Massachusetts! Also in my spare time and when possible I help people!

To change the subject and let you know, I might send another letter with some ideas on how to reduce traffic and accidents while helping the working-class people and using less oil, which could help you get votes. Senator John Kerry you are a man with morals and I wish you luck!!!

Sincerely, James C. Ferrari

The military-spokesman for 'Iraqi-freedom' campaign, blatantly says, something like, they're using psychological-warfare on the Iraqis, and then you realize if you notice, this happens daily on some television and media, I believe this is to purposely cause people stress so it's easier for the bad-rich people to hoard and control their ill-gotten fortunes, and not have to share with less fortunate peoples!

This is not equality, when they're manipulating people! At least the money-system, which is good for incentive purposes, should be more equal!, but it's not! In fact there is a class-warfare, money distribution is way unequal!!!! Decline in America's morals, the problem that will be the downfall, and only the wealthiest have the controls to fix this.

This old-divide and conquer attitude is creating kaos!!! This Iraq-occupation that the President George W. Bush has led, without the support of the United Nations has made enemies and lost allies and friendships, all for what?!!! This is a repeat of history, how stupid, fighting over land and the monies!

Positively I think that the President George W. Bush truly cares about the country, but it's wrong for the administration to prolong war, with escalation and more hatefulness! It's a tooth for a tooth not a tooth for ten! And what's the difference between a predatorial lion and a human being? Humans have the intelligence to be humane, hence humans.

The purpose of writing the sections about wars is because I care about America. I wanted to warn that pre-emptive strike could cause more problems, and added hatred.

And . . . ,

My stepfather, who was in the navy, would say "never back down from a fight," . . . 'but also never start a fight' he was alright. I live by the "golden rule" . . . "do unto others as you would have done to you". Now you see conflict, the kind sometimes using chemical poisons!!!? That's just sick. I would never poison a person, not for politics, not for my own money and fortune. Here's a fact, I've been so good, that is to people, when someone does me wrong and I've suffered . . . . something happens to them and they suffer also! Like carma, the golden rule in reverse, fate. And I didn't lift a finger, they did it themselves! I just want friendliness.

Be careful what you believe in the news

I was being abused by the company that I worked for on the days of the attack on the money towers. On the 3rd year of working for a wholesale auto parts business I became a manager lead-person. The first year was good, the district boss above myself let me run the show and I improved the place, being that I managed previous places, then they brought in a head hunting jerk from up-state New York, who fired others, used us as stepping stones, got himself a promotion, then after 8 months, fabricated and lied on paper about the good work I did, took away workers, and was adding work on myself when I was already multi-tasking, but he was trying to get me to resign so he could bring someone else in cheaper to do the job.

Add to that, that the fact is the last generation of people bought 30 yr. old homes for about $14,000, compared to families now buying a 60 yr. old home at about $140,000 that is rip-off high prices! Now add to that the approximate $1.00 per gallon added for gas, which cost about $1,000 extra per year on families across America, that is alleged, most likely filtered through the oil companies to pay for a war most people didn't want. I agree they had the right to take Saddam out of Iraq, but their mistake was to take the whole country . . . pre-emptive style, that's why there's resistance and counter attacks. War should be a last resort. Lastly, here's a fact, that our soldiers and workers still make good profits even during the peace times.

They need to stop the fighting, and also stop taking the financial securities from good, hard-working and peace-loving families.

After 3 years of the Iraq war, America's women mostly say, enough is enough, about 63% of Americans want to stop spending in Iraq and use money for America's people who were hit by more and bigger hurricanes than usual. And, the gas prices could be kept low to help average peoples! The men need to start bringing out the peace pipes!

Here's another letter written and sent by myself,

February 1, 2004

Dear Senator John Kerry,

Here is some information that you may use if you wish! Some Republicans on c-span said there was 300 million dollars cut from the intelligence budget and that Sen. Kerry had voted for this and . . . that is why attacks like the USS Cole happened!

I do not believe this, I think attacks happen because of overly-greedy, bad, and intrusive U.S. foreign policy! And what did the greedy Bush administration do for the first 8 months? . . . instead of going after Bin Laden, they were too busy deregulating nuclear, oil drilling, and industrial regulations for self-profit to take care of national security!!! Now George Bush was also weak on security.

Also, what lessons were even learned from September 11th?, the Bush administration has learned nothing?! They think more security, more spies, and pre-emptive war will fix this! Wrong! Do we really want to live spying on each other constantly, with loss of privacy, loss of liberties?!, not!

The lesson that we must learn from the attack on the money towers is not to be too greedy or too controlling in other countries!

Because if America sets an example of selfish greediness, then some countries will do the same! War begets war, . . . Peace begets peace!, thus . . .

If we set the example of putting people first!, . . . not money first, . . . then people first means less fighting over money and land!

Then spending for intelligence and security can be reduced, . . . with less worries, . . . less threats, . . . and more friendliness!!!!

This is why we must work together with our allies and other countries and not snub them! Also, mind our business and live and let live. Let's see, now that Saddam was weakened for ten years, and not a big threat, how come we don't see the number of innocent women and children killed in Iraq bombings. Is this pursuit of oil, military-position, and business contracts?!

Media is controlled, where is the accountability? Were fellow Americans killed for a business gain?

People need caring, sharing and kindness!

Here's a weird and ironic coincidence that I will share with you in these writings . . .

This terrible attack on the money-towers left many innocent-people, and not so innocent dead. This happens on Sept. 11th., many of us living witness this . . . .

and . . . It just so happens my birthday is on Sept. 10th., and my wife and I have Sept. 12th. as our wedding anniversary!

For me personally this has an odd timing like a twist of fate! Because from 10 years ago-plus, I was suffering stress from over-working, multi-tasking, to survive the rip-off economy! After my wife and I bought a 60-year old house for 90,000, plus intrest,! Having 60,000.00 a year isn't enough?! I had to be a "jack of most trades', and was overloaded with too-many worries! But now this twist of fate turns the tables and even the richest have the worries!!! I wrote many times about the over-load of the average families! Finally I wrote a book, not yet published, about decline in morals! Then in 2002 I almost had a stroke and ended up on pills! I am a straight-A student and a peaceful man. The high-prices have caused too-much stressfulness!

Good luck, James C. Ferrari
1865 Roosevelt, Ave
Springfield, Mass

One more letter written and sent by myself;

Presentation,　　　　　　　　　　　June 03, 2003

This is a suggestion that a type of car-pooling will be created using 9-19 passenger-vans, for average people going to work, ect., for less than cab-fair and . . . , door to door!

Which is a win, win, win situation, creates less-traffic, which makes roads safer for our children! Rookie-drivers have to deal with much more traffic than we did! Something like . . . 3,800 people died in a year from terrorism . . . , yet about 40,000 people died from traffic-accidents!!! And if Americans do the right-thing by car-pooling, we will use much less oil, and other countries will see we are setting a good-example by conserving oil. Also this reduces pollution! And obviously sells lots of the 9-19 passenger vans. Some people who can't afford that second-car will be thrilled to save a few-bucks! Less roadwork! The government will save money. Right now there are more 30-40 car pile-ups than ever! Less accidents means less liabilities! A persons' car breaks down, they could use the van to get to work! But most important is the protection of our kids!

James C. Ferrari
Springfield, Mass.

It's now March 14th, 2006, and have you been indoctrinated, have you been persuaded to be a selfish, cold bitch like themselves? Don't believe the program that wants you to work like them, blaming, and kicking out fellow team-mates, with a persecution, against a good person.

And also with that.

This is a fact that a kid put cleaning chemicals in a teachers' drink! That's not a prank, or being punked, that is poisoning!

What the heck are these kids learning off the games and media? To be sick bastards!!!? Thankfully I have morals.

A true story I was with some friends about thirty years ago having a few drinks in a backyard. There was this man that thought he was big and bad cause he knew some karate. He started a fight and he punched me in face, when I was turned, he did not budge me but he kept trying to hit.

A minute passes.

I became ticked off and after blocking his kicks and punches, I hit him once right in the head and he went down. I held him still with my hands, my buddies said "keep pounding him", but I did not, he said he would stop, and I showed him some mercy. If I kept hitting it would have been revenge back and forth. But instead he gave an apology a week later and that was the end of the fights.

Now imagine a society that makes and purchases just what is needed, with a few frivolities, no beat the clock, much less stress, work not for the greater good but for the common good, with good enjoyment and fun. I'm not against capitolism, but the overly high prices. Not against technology but use of too many electronic devices, even if efficient, is a waste of energies. Not against cars but the accidents and pollution from too many cars. And kids in cars that watch the electronics instead of the road, need safety limits.

Like taking candy from a baby, that's a businessman saying, but it's not moral. I feel cheated and the fact after working for years they've given "just too much", of my tax dollars away, so that some on welfare checks have college, and pass us and yet I can't afford college!

They've taken too much.

And we've, worked for that money, it's not theirs. Taking from my kids. It's no secret and many people know, and do boycott, and I am against a type of politician with a support of immoral high taxes and prices.

Now let's write about the fact that legal law should be the morals kind, not used for manipulation. Some laws today with the design to force a person to buy something is just dictatorship. If it's a safety issue that's different. And sometimes they do not make a law, so as not to disturb sales of a new product even safety is put to the side . . . ;

That's a disrespect. Here's a supposed law that forces a dad, who pays support, to pay for college for a kid after they're an adult 18-23, yet no one can force him to pay for college for the other adult kid that lives with him! The dad pays for the kids college only if he can afford this.

Some politicians don't care the fact is they let people and kids drive the cars, while using a cell phone, so as not to disrupt sales, when accidents did happen because no laws and no safety restrictions were put into place. Now they put some. And using computers while driving the cars, and dvd players, is a risk to people and kids. Where's the safety laws?!!! Stereos are probably best. Some modern devices need a dictation of the safety laws.

The fact truly is that others decisions have affected my life, too many times!

My fathers' abandonment, and then I am forced to learn a lot myself, and end up in the poor section.

And . . . ,

My stepfather's an alcholic that is sometimes alright. I was not taught the diligent toothcare and lost some teeth, just as a teen boy. Then as a man the prices are boosted way high. Sometimes when people medal with things, they ruin them. Like porn was decent, the slight addiction of the adults, I would have beat some years-ago!,. and classic is best. Today the fact is that the public television has too little censorship, the public television has the fighting propaganda, television with morals is the best. Have a little compassion. A word of advice, that is to 'leave well enough alone'. Have morals and allow the freedom of the peoples.

Because of today's deception, the best thing you can do is 'read between the lies', when watching the news!, and reading some newspapers! There is a lot of propaganda and bias! A good relationship depends on trust and truthfulness, the same is true of many aspects of living.

Next, here is a brief, 'ten years after', recap of the previous chapters;

1. Education . . . today our children sadly know more about fictional-cartoon game characters and shoot-em up fighting games than their school-work, all to sell more crap and waste electricity, . . . wrong path!

2. Sex and pornography . . . . prostitution is legal in Nevada?, and immoral rich and poor business-men, who should earn the reward of love and sex through a show of goodness, now just pay for this! Akin to slavery, they can buy a person!, prostitution sells immorality and steps over the line too much!

3. Crime . . . . Sept. 11th, if this is a modern-society then why do we see a repeat of history?!, . . . fighting over money and land!!!

4. Drugs . . . . there may be less drug use, but with over-complicated rules set down by the rich-dictatorship, it's a wonder our kids don't use drugs!

5. The break-up of the American family too-much stress caused by the rip-off prices!

6. Over taxation and Monarchy? . . . . the wealthiest people just got like a 4%-plus tax break by the special-interest president, while the American families have too—much stress caused by high rip-off prices while wondering if their jobs will be replaced by technology or Mexicans!

7. Spoiled-rotten!, . . . Enron! Nowadays the bank robs you!

8. All talk but no action!, ... "Change is good", but only if it sells something, they don't want to change to do the right-things!

9. . . . . "America the beautiful", . . . If selling to-much un-necessities and creating more garbage, just to sell something, and the pollution of more cars than we really need is progress, then maybe it's time to change and set a better example for our children and other countries, and really keep America beautiful and natural.

10. The American scheme . . . . Enron!

11. Preventative medicine and healthcare . . . . and this I've seen progress, thank god, but needs lots more honest-programs. Sen. John F. Kerry supports this and prevention is the best.
12. A living history of the next 10yrs . . . . Americans need improvement too, that's for damn sure, especially the richest, greediest trouble-makers! We need rich people and poor people who are sharing and caring towards the common good!

A short-page, . . . suggestion; that to reduce the amount of criminals, any foreigners who have a record, or get a criminal record with in a few years, cannot stay in this country, but must be sent back.

To end this book, the thing I would like to see happen is this country of America to be a leader by setting good examples for other countries! Less competition added friendliness

Would America, someday, put aside the ego and let another country be #1, if peacefulness among countries is honorable and can be trusted?!

And will the production of things take the direction of what we need!, . . . not useless bullshit sold just to move numbers?!

Lastly, instead of trying to create starwar/Kaos propaganda, how about using money to learn how to produce enough food for all good people on earth! This will lead to a true 'Peace on earth', America is a country that is in a position to help accomplish this!!! I create peacefulness.

Last, not least . . .

I teach kids togetherness . . . , the truth shall set us free, and godbless all good peoples!

Thanks

Survey Questions;

As a concerned American, do you agree . . .

1.) That there is too much computer made illusions, on television, and that they flash too many scenes too fast, which is not good for your eyes or mind?

   Yes___ No___ tips___

2.) That some censorship is needed and television should be made more simple again, so our learning children won't be subjected to too much illusion?

   Yes___ No___ tips___

3.) That pornography be limited and censored to protect our children's future?

   Yes___ No___ tips___

4.) That crime could be reduced if there were more jobs and better pay for people?

   Yes___ No___ tips___

5.) That the best way to stop drug use is to, rehabilitate drug users, not to wage costly drug wars?

   Yes___ No___ tips___

6.) That American government is almost becoming a "monarchy" with its over-taxation of the poor and middle class?

   Yes___ No___ tips___

7.) That our children and families are suffering difficulties as a result of both parents having to work full-time?

Yes____ No____ tips____

8.) That Americans are too obsessed with movies, fiction and that we should put our time and money into helping the real world?

Yes____ No____ tips____

9.) That the space exploration be done just for the satellites we need for earth, maintenance, etc. And the money saved from such limitation, be used for us here on earth?

Yes____ No____ tips____

10.) That censorship is needed in the violent fighting war movies

Yes____ No____ tips____

11.) That a lot of Americans are getting spoiled rotten, when they should live more modestly, when so many others don't have even the basic necessities?

Yes____ No____ tips____

12.) That Americans need to do these things if we are to continue to be a good example to ourselves and other countries!

Yes____ No____ tips____

Please fill out this survey and send it to your nearest senator, please make your opinions count!

Writers' . . . , the authors page

My name is James C. Ferrari, though I drive like an old lady! I'm Italian, Canadian . . . French, and a little Black-foot Indian. Part of myself indeed was in America before any others. I was supposed to go to college, my art teacher wanted me to go, but never made it. Instead I was supporting the 1st of my children at the age of about 19. I used to paint and sell portraits of people and pets in my late teens and early twenties. I have a portfolio, and sometimes still do artwork.

Though I have a rich name and ancestry of teachers, musicians, and artisans, was brought up in the poor section of Holyoke, Mass. Where as children, my sis, my mom, and myself had to endure the abuse of my stepfather, when he was sober he was a saintly man. But, an alcoholic, when drunk was so abusive to the point of having to have him arrested several times. Like "Dr. Jekyel and Mr. Hyde", in public people thought he was normal. But he had problems. It's too bad, he was at times a decent person. I felt sorry for the man, but violence should be a defensive last resort, and I feel his aggressions were because he worked too much! He had happiness sometimes.

I went from a very tough life as a kid, cried many times, and laughed on occasions, only to grow-up to an economy where the business owners, who use to set fair and just prices, now have created, many of them, get rich quick overly inflated prices. Last generation parents bought a 30 yr. old house for about 14,000, now a 60-yr. old house is about 149,000! I've worked so hard to beat this economy, that I became damaged, now I'm almost back to normal, and this book is about prevention, thanks.